AVA-THE ALGORITHM FOR CRACKING COMPETITIVE EXAMS

(JEE, NEET, ICRA, JET, UPSC, GATE, CAT, NTSE, KVPY, OLYMPIADS)

ACHARYA VISHVENDRA

Dedicated to the complexities during my preparation for JEE, leading to decoded algorithm for cracking competitve exams which helped me to get admission in government engineering college,college of technology,pantnagar,uttrakhand through JEE(M)/AIEEE

Contents

Foreword

This book is a Small effort with the vision of "DEVELOPING MIND,DEVELOP INDIA" by developing young minds to crack competitive exam,getting admission in a good college,fetch a good job & being successful in personal,academic,& professional dimensions of life.

Preface

During my preparation of JEE(JOINT ENTRANCE EXAM),i struggled a lot to learn the process of solving problems.i soon realised that my past learning during my schooling is not sufficient to solve problems.

during schooling there was a limited information & limited protype based questions.on an average a chapter had 3 or 4 formulas on an average & i could solve most of the questions using only those 3 or 4 formulas because all questions were based on same prototypes.Revising those limited formulas again & again gave me enough confidence to score good in school.

But this strategy didn't work while solving JEE BOOKS like:

H.C.VERMA,I.E.IRODOV,D.C.PANDEY,RASNICK HALLIDAY IN PHYSICS

A.DAS GUPTA,HALL & KNIGHT,S.L.LONEY,R.D.SHARMA ETC. IN MATHEMATICS

INORGANIC CHEMISTRY BY J.D.LEE,PHYSICAL CHEMISTRY BY DR.P.BAHADUR

ORGANIC CHEMISTRY BY MORRISON & BOYD ETC.

i was very comfortable with natural thinking,i had a lot of questions in my mind like what is fundamental source of information in books.who made laws?why things work in a particular pattern?why there are boundations & limitations?

But solving questions was not that easy.i tried different patterns,i consulted my friends,teachers,relatives but they told their own stories and i got more confused.soon i realised that asking questions is very easy but finding answers is very tough.when i found no solutions to my problem i decided to find myself how to solve questions by experiments rather than working on somebody's suggestions.

i observed my friends who were able to solve questions and tried to find why they are able to solve questions & not me.i compared their working with mine.i tried to find which books they are using,which questions they are solving.i bought the books but still no solution.

i then observed my teachers why they are able to solve questions & not me?i found that most of the teachers area able to solve most of the questions from the book that they have.but when i asked something new,even they were unable to answer.then i realised that nobody is there who can answer every question.everybody has just developed a system in which they have practised a lot of prototype based questions & after a certain time prototypes are repeated.you just need to analyse the process of solving problems and your emotions/energy and learn the patterns of solving questions.you also have to learn the pattern that your "MIND-BRAIN SYSTEM" follows,when you learn to solve problems.If you can develop some mental powers(strong will power, deep concentration power, power to achieve silent mind, sharp memory power, power of sharp problem solving skills, sharp analytical skill power, sharp optimal performance power) in you,then cracking competitive exam is your cup of tea.

There are only a few things which are to be practised and when you practice them with a strong will power,analysis & recursively updated strategies in tests you can score good.For instance most of the questions of kinematics can be solved by just using 3 equations & their menifestations.

But this all consumed a lot of my time & energy and i was just able to crack JEE(M)/AIEEE with a decent rank and i got admission in government college of technology,pantnagar,uttrakhand in the decent branch of I.T.(information technology).although it was very little as compared to my heart breaking efforts but still i was able to get an opportunity to join a government college from where i could hope for a good career.

But i was never satisfied with my result.i thought to do something which can help others to choose the optimal path of preparing for competitive exams.so that their energy & time is not wasted in changing strategies,methods and procedures and it is optimally utilised in preparing for exam rather than experiments.

In a nutshell we can say that there are 3 mutually exclusive dimensions of working for cracking competitive exams.these are

1.Information

2.Process

3.Energy/emotion/mental powers

This book is an effort to discuss the process of cracking competitive exam in an elaborative way,the problems during the process & dealing strategies in the form of an algorithm so that you can work on all of these 3 dimensions,crack your competitive exam,get admission in a decent college,get your dream job or start your own business,achieve success & can contribute to the vision of

"DEVELOPING MIND,DEVELOP INDIA"

Acknowledgements

Thanks to the omnipresent frequencies for stimulating my frequencies to decode the process of solving

Prologue

The universe is following quantized rules.Success & failures are concerned with decoding these rules.This book is elaboration of decoded rules for cracking competitive exams.

The basis of decoding these rules is my experience as a student while preparing for JEE,cracking JEE(M)/AIEEE,getting admission in government engineering college,college of technology,pantnagar,uttrakhand.successfully completing my engineering in information technology,getting a decent job as a physics faculty for JEE & NEET in reputed coaching institutes of delhi and 11 years of my experience with thousands of students as a physics faculty in reputed coaching institutes of delhi & kota for JEE & NEET.

CHAPTER ONE

INTRODUCTION

1.1:COMPETITIVE EXAMS IN INDIA:

For a **lower & middle class family student** in our country india,the most **optimised option** for living a better life is to **crack competitive exam**.

FIG:1.1: A LOWER MIDDLE CLASS FAMILY IN INDIA

Every year more than 3 crore aspirants prepare for competitive exams like **JEE, NEET,UPSC,GATE,SSC and banking.**
*(source:https://yourstory.com/2019/07/edtech-tier-ii-iii-cities-competitive-exams/amp).

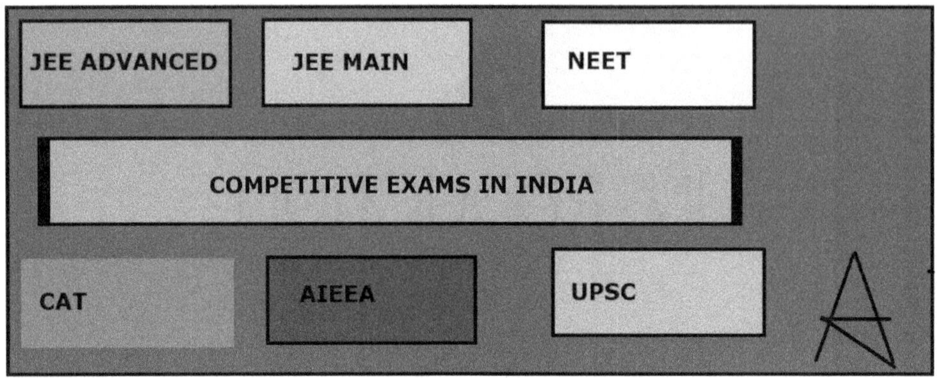

FIG:1.2: COMPETITIVE EXAMS IN INDIA

1.2: SOME STATISTICS:

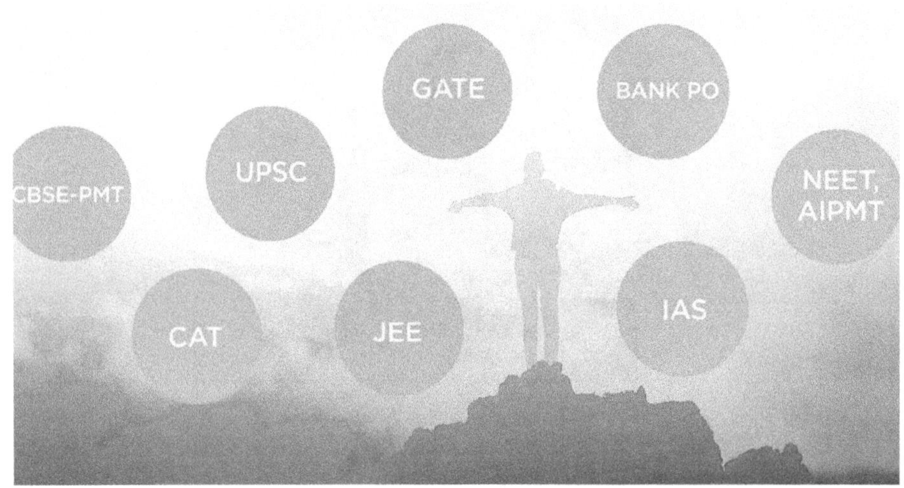

FIG:1.3 : SOME STATISTICS ABOUT COMPETITIVE EXAMS IN INDIA

JEE ADVANCED 2021:

A total of 1,41,699 candidates appeared in both paper 1 and 2 of the JEE (Advanced) Exam 2021. As many as 41,862 candidates have qualified the JEE-(Advanced) 2021, of which 6,452 are girls. JEE Advanced exam was conducted on October 3 for seeking admission to 23 IITs across the country

JEE MAINS 2021:

Of over 10.48 lakh students who applied to appear for JEE Main results including all four sessions, as many as 9,39,008 took the exam.Students who make it to the top 2.5 lakh spots in JEE Main will be selected for JEE Advanced.

NEET 2021:

A total of 14,10,755 appeared in NEET UG 2021 exam, among these 7,97,042 candidates have qualified .

UPSC 2021:

A total of 10,93,984 candidates applied for this examination, out of which 5,08,619 candidates appeared,

A total of 685 candidates - 508 men and 177 women - have qualified and they have been recommended by the Commission for appointment to various central services

1.3:SEATS IN ENGINEERING & MEDICAL COLLEGES IN INDIA:

FIG. 1.4: ENGINEERING COLLEGES IN INDIA

FIG. 1.5: MEDICAL COLLEGES IN INDIA

As of 2021, the total number of seats for undergraduate programs is 23,997 and for postgraduate programs 13,664 in all the 31 NITs put together

As of 2021, the total number of seats for undergraduate programs in all IITs is 16,234.

there are about 24000 Govt. medical college MBBS seats in our country.

1.4:ACCEPTANCE RATES IN IITS,NITS,& MBBS COLLEGES IN INDIA

FIG. 1.6: ACCEPTANCE RATE IN COMPETITIVE EXAMS

1.4.1. IN IITS:

Admission to IITs is extremely difficult. Only the top 1.54 percent of the applicants are admitted.

1.4.2. IN NITS:

These institutes are among the top-ranked engineering colleges in India and have one of the lowest acceptance rates for engineering institutes, of about 2.2 percent.

1.4.3. IN NEET GOVT. MBBS COLLEGES:

acceptance rates for mbbs is about 1.7 percent.

1.5:THE ANALYSIS:

FIG. 1.7: THE ANALYSIS

From the above statistics we can analyse that success rate in competitive exams and getting admission in top colleges is extremly difficult.(about 1.54 percent for IIT,about 2.2 percent for NIT and about 5.7 percent for NEET)

FIG. 1.8: CRACKING COMPETITIVE EXAM IS EXTREMLY DIFFICULT

Now the question arises **"is there something special in students who gets successful in competitive exams and gets admissions in these colleges?"**.The answer is **"yes"**.They have a better **"MIND-BRAIN SYSTEM"** than rest of the students.

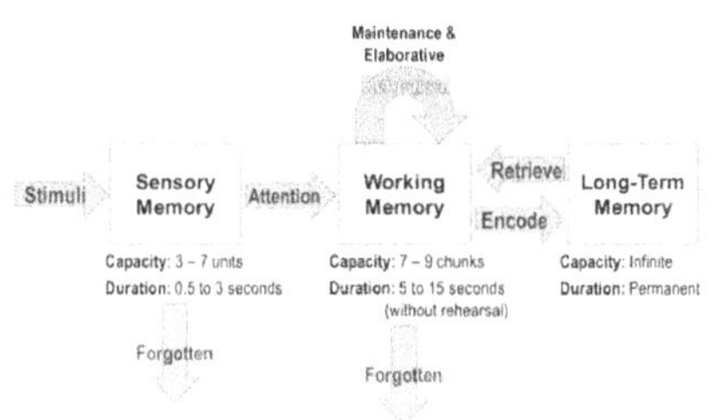

FIG. 1.9: WORKING MODEL OF "MIND-BRAIN SYSTEM"

Their **information processing capabilities,algorithms & mental powers**(strong will power,deep concentration power,silent mind power,sharp memory power,power of sharp problem solving skills,power of sharp analytical skills & power of optimal performance)are better than rest of the students.

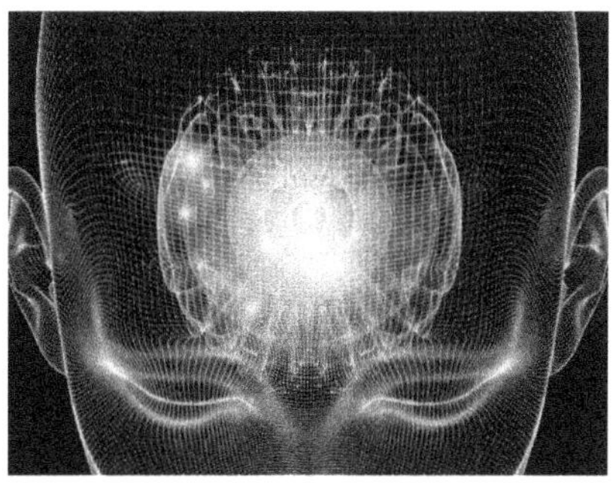

FIG. 1.10: MENTAL POWERS OF SUCCESSFUL STUDENTS

But the good point is that(for average students leaving exceptional students)these **information processing capabilities , algorithms** & **mental powers** can be developed and improved by proper **TRAINING PROGRAMS** as discussed in section 1.11)

so if you feel that you don't have these **capabilities and mental powers**,first of all develop these **capabiltities and mental powers** before start preparing for competitive exams.

thats why most of the students are unable to **crack competitive exams** because they only **gatherinformation from books** but don't have **information processing capabilities , algorithms** & **mental powers**

FIG. 1.11: WHY MOST OF TUDENTS FAIL TO CRACK COMPETITIVE EXAMS

so if you are aspiring to crack competitive exams first of all learn and develop these **information processing capabilities,algorithms** & **mental powers.**

This book is specifically written for developing and learning the information processing capabilities & algorithms with a basic introductin to mental powers.but if you aspire to develop and learn explicitly mental powers you can

refer to my book
"OST-DEVELOPING MIND,DEVELOP INDIA",CHAPTER-6:MIND TRAINING PROGRAMS".
This book is available on amazon,flipcart and notionpress.
you can purchase it online by searching
""OST-DEVELOPING MIND,DEVELOP INDIA" or by searching"ACHARYA VISHVENDRA"

FIG. 1.12: OST-DEVELOPING MIND-DEVELOP INDIA

1.6:DIMENSIONS OF STUDENT:

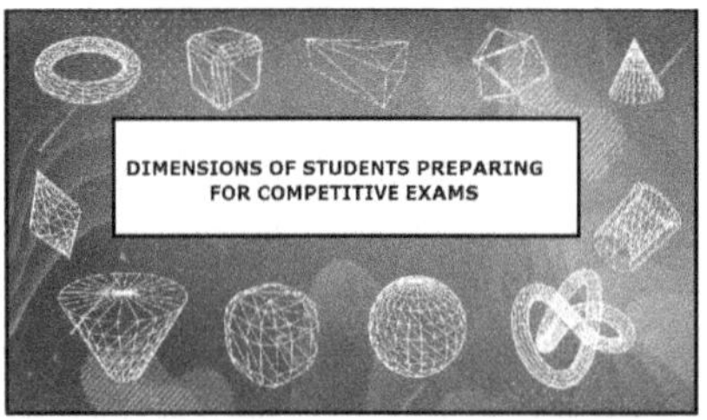

FIG. 1.13: DIMENSIONS OF STUDENT

Any student has 3 dimensions with respect to his preparation for competitive exams
1.The brain 2.The mind 3.The energy

FIG. 1.14: BRAIN,MIND & ENERGY

1.7:THE BRAIN:

Brain is the central organ in human body.It is composed of billions of neurons that communicate with each other in the form of a network having trillions of connections called synapses,

Human brain is the most complex organs in our body.

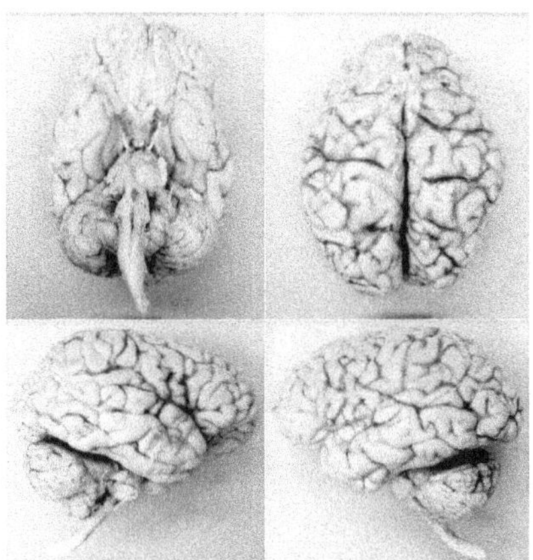

FIG.1.15: THE HUMAN BRAIN

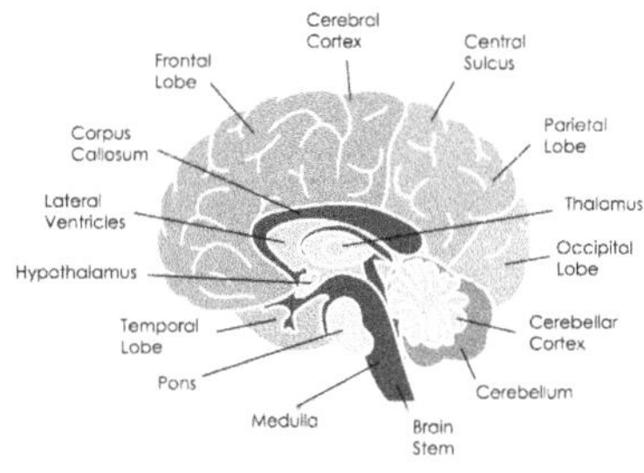

FIG. 1.16: SCHEMATIC DIAGRAM OF THE BRAIN

On the basis of an experiment over about 8000 brains it was observed that the average brain weight of the adult male was 1336 gr; for the adult female 1198 gr. With increasing age, brain weight decreases by 2.7 gr in males, and by 2.2 gr in females per year.

(source:https://pubmed.ncbi.nlm.nih.gov/ 8072950/#:~:text=The%20average%20brain%20weight%20of,gr%20in%20females%20per%20year.)

1.8:THE MIND:

Sigmund Freud was an Austrian neurologist and the founder of psychoanalysis, a clinical method for evaluating and treating pathologies in the psyche through dialogue between a patient and a psychoanalyst.

(source:https://en.wikipedia.org/wiki/Sigmund_Freud)

In the illustration below is Freud's division of these three levels and the estimated usage of each level. They are the conscious, subconscious, and unconscious. Working together they create our reality.

(source:http://journalpsyche.org/understanding-the-human-mind/)

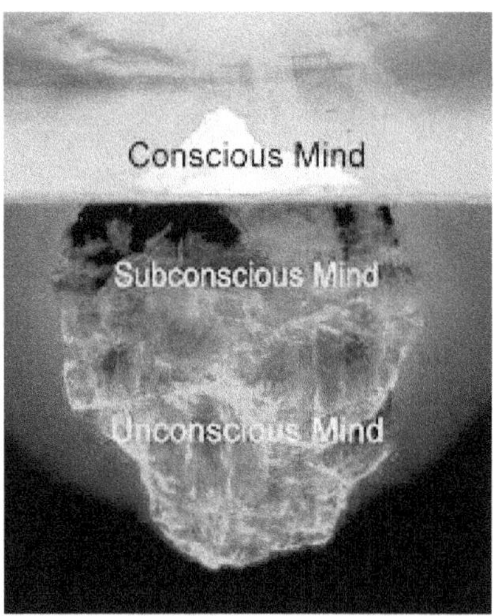

FIG.1.17: 3 LEVELS OF HUMAN MIND AS PROPOSED BY SIGMUND FREUD

to know more about human mind you can refer the book "OST-DEVELOPING MIND,DEVELOP INDIA"-CHAPTER-3:MIND BRAIN SYSTEM.This book can be purchased online from amazon and flipcart by searching the title "OST-DEVELOPING MIND,DEVELOP INDIA".

1.9:THE ENERGY:

1.9.1:KUNDALINI POWER:

Apart from biological energies which are necessary for the biological processes,humans also posses another metaphysica; energy which is concenred with higher dimensions of life.

There is always a quest inside us to be better in life.This quest is because of this metaphysical energy.This energy in inactive form is called "KUNDALINI POWER".

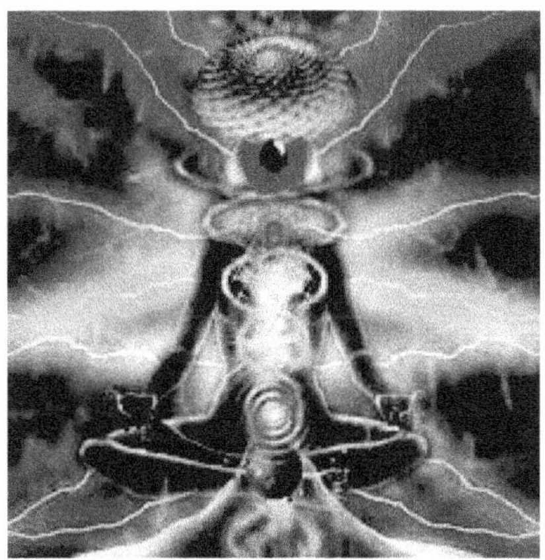

FIG. 1.18: KUNDALINI SHAKTI ACTIVATION

1.9.2: HUMAN CHAKRA SYSTEM:

Theory of Human chakra system was developed in India between 1500 and 500 BC in the oldest text called the Vedas.

Evidence of chakras, spelled cakra, is also found in the Shri Jabala Darshana Upanishad, the Cudamini Upanishad, the Yoga-Shikka Upanishad and the Shandilya Upanishad. According to the scholar Anodea Judith in her book the Wheels of Life

(source:https://indigomassagetherapy.com/uncategorized/what-is-the-origin-of-the-chakra-system/)

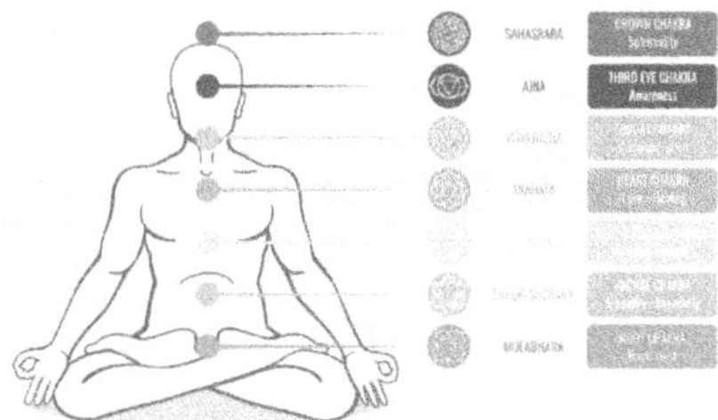

FIG 1.19:HUMAN CHAKRA SYSTEM

1.9.3:THE PURPOSE OF KUNDALINI POWER:

Just observe yourself and feel the tendency of being better in life.you may be having will to score better in exam or to earn money or to buy a new motorbike or new car.

This tendency is always toward betterment or higher dimensions.

in terms of higher dimensions of metaphysical experience we can say that kundalini has the tendency to reach to higher dimensions or chakras.

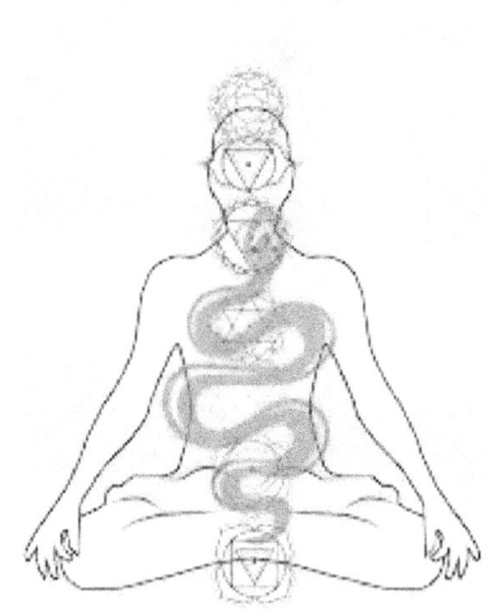

FIG 1.20:KUNDALINI SHAKTI MOVEMENT FROM LOWER TO HIGHER ENERGY CENTRES

1.10: THE MIND-BRAIN SYSTEM:

These 3 works together as a system called as the **"MIND-BRAIN SYSTEM"**.

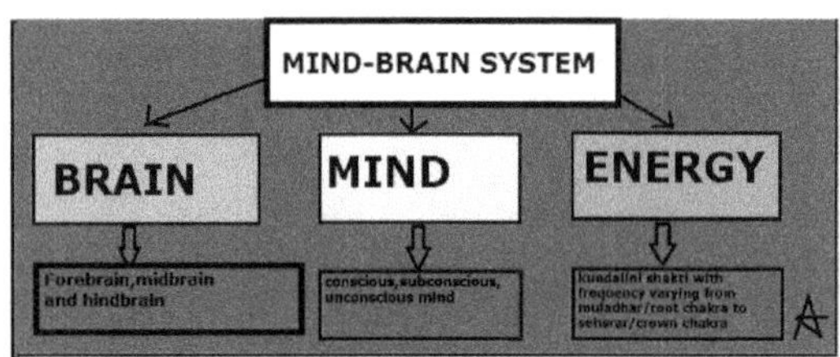

FIG. 1.21: MIND-BRAIN SYSTEM

(for details about "MIND-BRAIN SYSTEM" you can read the book"DEVELOPING MIND-DEVELOP INDIA",CHAPTER-3)

It can be purchased online on amazon and flipcart by searching its title "DEVELOPING MIND-DEVELOP INDIA")

you can also go through the book "OST-DEVELOPING MIND,DEVELOP INDIA"-CHAPTER-6:MIND TRAINING PROGRAMS

This book can be purchased online from amazon and flipcart by searching the title

"OST-DEVELOPING MIND,DEVELOP INDIA"

FIG. 1.22: SNAPSHOT OF AMAZON.IN FOR THE BOOK OST-DEVELOPING MIND,DEVELOP INDIA

1.11:WHY STUDENTS OF SAME TEACHER ACHIEVE DIFFERENT RESULTS?

FIG. 1.23: WHY STUDENTS OF SAME TEACHER ACHIEVE DIFFERENT RESULTS?

if we analyse the "MIND-BRAIN SYSTEM" of the student as an **informatio processing device** then input here is same for all then why we have differen outputs?

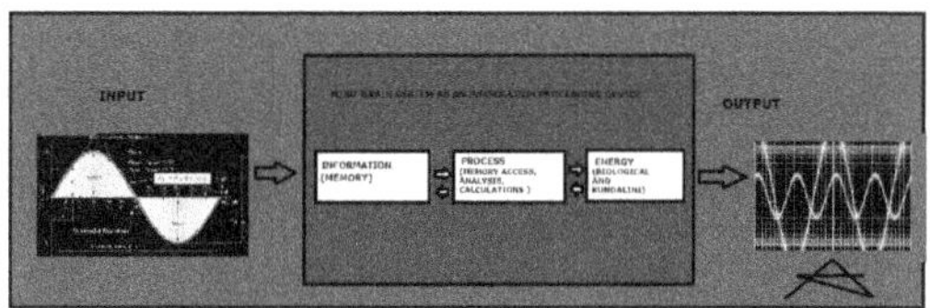

FIG. 1.24: MIND-BRAIN SYSTEM AS AN INFORMATION PROCESSING DEVICE

The reason for this is that students have different mental abilities.

FIG. 1.25: STUDENTS HAVE DIFFERENT MENTAL CAPABILITIES

Based on research conducted at the University of Granada, it has been known that these abilities can be improved by planned training.

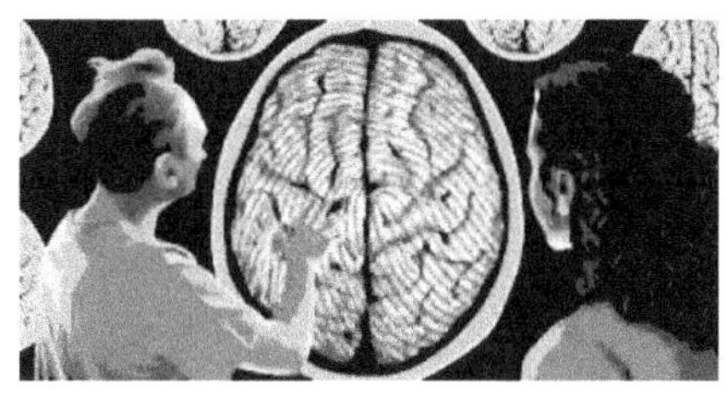

FIG. 1.26: MENTAL CAPABILITES CAN BE IMPROVED BY TRAINING

(source:https://www.sciencedaily.com/releases/2018/12/181211103108.htm)

1.12: HAVE A SILENT & POWERFUL "MIND-BRAIN SYSTEM"

So before proceeding to the next chapter make sure you have a silent and powerful **"MIND-BRAIN SYSTEM"**.if you are unable to have that yourself we can help you out.

you can also go through the book **"OST-DEVELOPING MIND,DEVELOP INDIA"-CHAPTER-6:MIND TRAINING PROGRAMS**

This book can be purchased online from amazon,flipcart & notionpress by searching the title

"OST-DEVELOPING MIND,DEVELOP INDIA"

It is developed by years of experiments and analysis of thousands of students and teachers.

just go through it and have a silent & powerful "MIND-BRAIN SYSTEM".

CHAPTER TWO

THE ALGORITHM

THE "MIND-BRAIN SYSTEM" of each studentsfollows an algorithm.

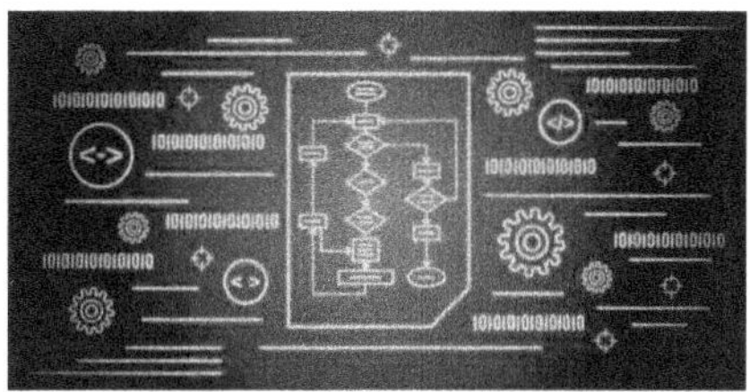

FIG 2.1:THE ALGORITHM OF "MIND-BRAIN SYSTEM"

Successful students uses strong & complex algorithm whereas unsuccessful students follows weak & simple algorithm.

FIG 2.2:SUCCESSFUL & UNSUCCESSFUL STUDENT

FIG. 2.3:SUCCESSFUL STUDENTS USE STRONG AND COMPLEX ALGORITHMS

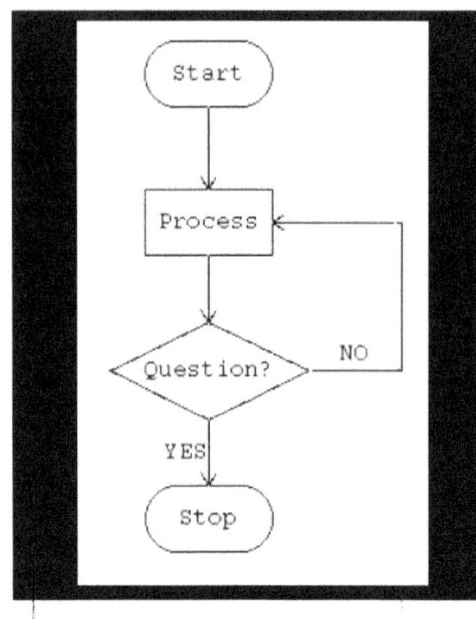

FIG. 2.4:UNSUCCESSFUL STUDENTS USE WEAK AND SIMPLE ALGORITHMS

with proper **"MIND-TRAINING PROGRAM"** students can gradually learn to develop strong and complex algorithms.

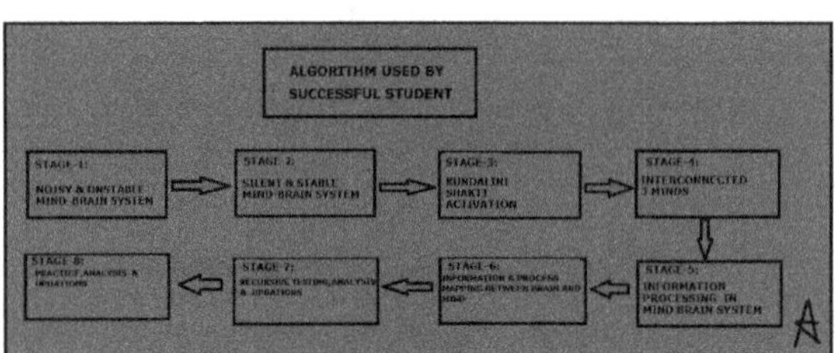

FIG 2.5: ALGORITHM USED BY SUCCESSFUL STUDENTS

So if you aspire to crack competitive exams then first of all learn the algorithms of **"MIND-BRAIN SYSTEM"** let's discuss it in details:

1.STAGE-1:NOISY AND UNSTABLE MIND-BRAIN SYSTEM:

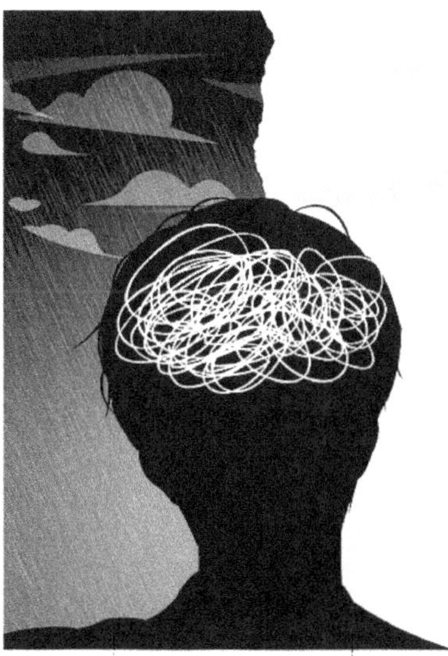

FIG. 2.6:NOISY & UNSTABLE "MIND-BRAIN SYSTEM"

Generally an average student has a noisy and unstable mind-brain system.They have unstable thoughts.They just reactcts to the thoughts which creates another thought and utimately a chain reaction is created. They gets trapped in the chain of thoughts.

This is quite natural and we don't need to be worried just try to focus on your work and gradually unstable thoughts will vanish and we will have a stable mind-brain system.

2.STAGE-2:SILENT AND STABLE MIND-BRAIN SYSTEM:

FIG. 2.7:SILENT AND STABLE MIND-BRAIN SYSTEM:

You have a silent and stable "MIND-BRAIN SYSTEM"now.you feel thoghtlessness and are able to focus much better on our work.Maintain yourself in this state.Thoghts will try to trap you but use will power to maintain your focus.Have a strong mind.if you will loose focus you will loose everything and will just struggle with thoughts.

STAGE-3:KUNDALINI SHAKTI ACTIVATION:

FIG. 2.8:KUNDALINI SHAKTI ACTIVATION:

Energy is fundamental prerequisite to create anything.So before aspiring to achieve anything you must have enough posiive energy in your "MIND-BRAIN SYSTEM" otherwise negative energy will trap you in illusions and you will loose focus and will not be able to get the desired result.

FIG.2.9:TRAP OF NEGATIVE ENERGY

STAGE4:INTERCONNECTED CONSCIOUS,SUBCONSCIOUS & UNCONSCIOUS MINDS:

FIG. 2.10:CONSCIOUS,UNCONSCIOUS & SUBCONSCIUS MIND

Interconnect your **CONSCIOUS,UNCONSCIOUS & SUBCONSCIUS MIND**

Just start studying **first line** of your chapter.The information contained in this line will first reach to your **sensory memory**(mapped with **conscious mind**),then **temporary memory**(mapped with **sub-conscious mind**) then permanent memory(mapped with **un-conscious mind).**

FIG. 2.11: THE PROCESS OF STUDYING

STAGE-5:INFORMATION PROCESSING IN MIND-BRAIN SYSTEM:

when you start studying, the following processes occurs in your **"MIND-BRAIN SYSTEM"**.

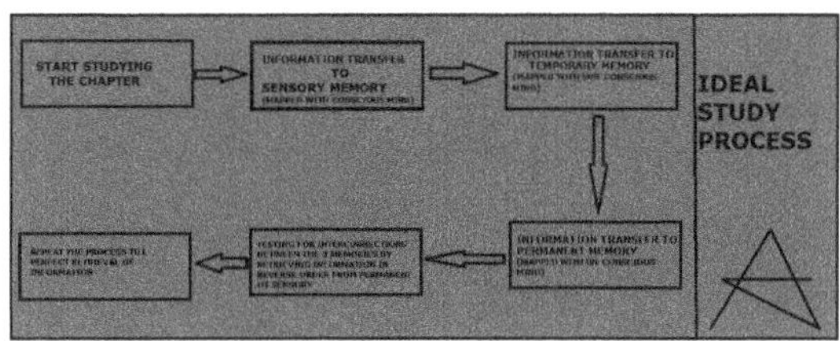

FIG. 2.12:INFORMATION PROCESSING IN MIND-BRAIN SYSTEM:

A sccessful student **completes** the entire process with **unbroken focus and determination** whereas unsuccessful student loses **focus in between** and is trapped in thoughts.

so the key point is **don't leave** in between.complete the **entire process**.if you will give up in any **intermediate step** you will be unable to **retrieve information from unconscious mind(Permanent memory)** when you will need it.

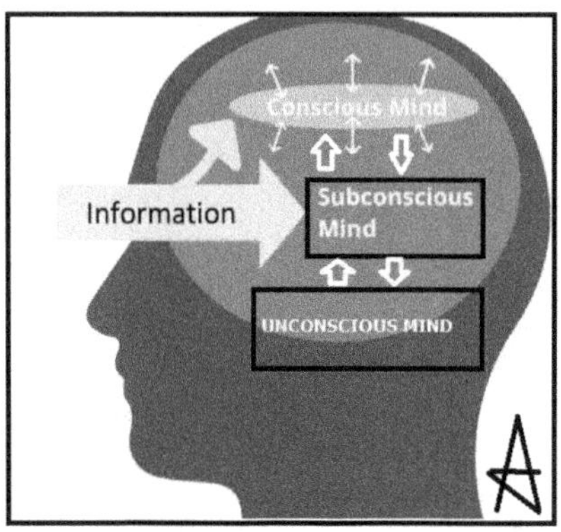

FIG. 2.13:CONSCIOUS,UNCONSCIOUS & SUBCONSCIUS MIND

As you must have seen that when you appear for exam then success and failure is due to retrieval of information from unconscious mind.

FIG. 2.14:UNSUCCESSFUL STUDENTS ARE UNABLE TO RETRIEVE INFORMATION DURING EXAM

FIG. 2.15:SUCCESSFUL STUDENTS ARE ABLE TO RETRIEVE INFORMATION DURING EXAM

you will be successful if you are able to retrieve information from unconscious mind and unsuccessful if you are unable to retrieve information.

hence the entire turning point behind successful and unsuccessful student is the **retrieval process of information from unconscious mind(PERMANENT MEMORY)**

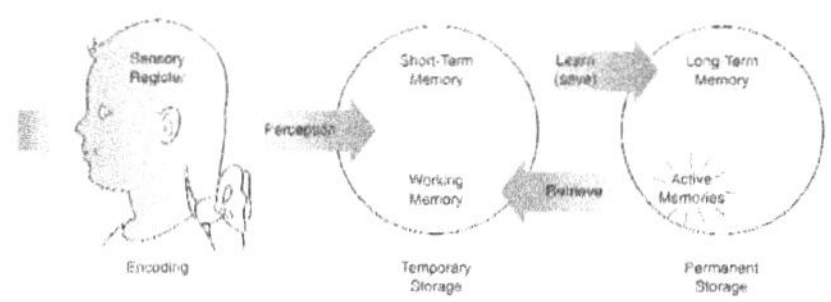

FIG. 2.16:INFORMATION PROCESSING IN MIND-BRAIN SYSTEM

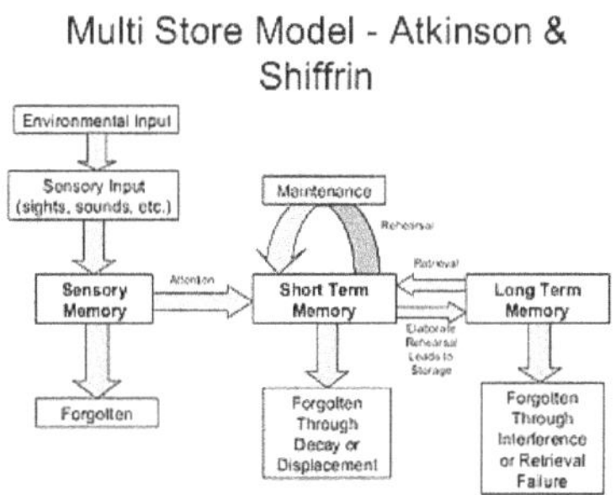

FIG. 2.17:ATKINSON & SHIFFRIN MODEL

Hence achieve mastery in the entire process and gradually you will learn how to store and retrieve information form your "MIND-BRAIN SYSTEM"which is the fundamental skill to successfully crack your exam.

STAGE-6:INFORMATION & PROCESS MAPPING BETWEEN BRAIN & MIND:

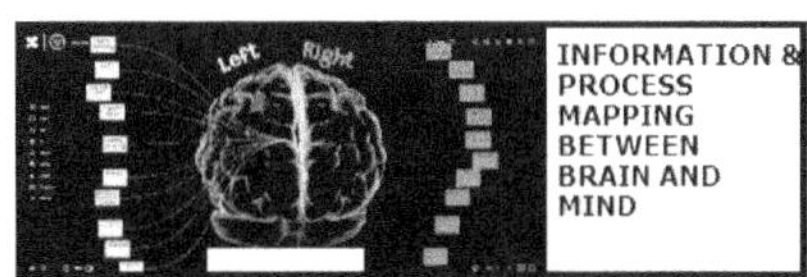

FIG. 2.18:INFORMATION & PROCESS MAPPING BETWEEN BRAIN & MIND

Information & process gets mapped between brain and mind as follows:

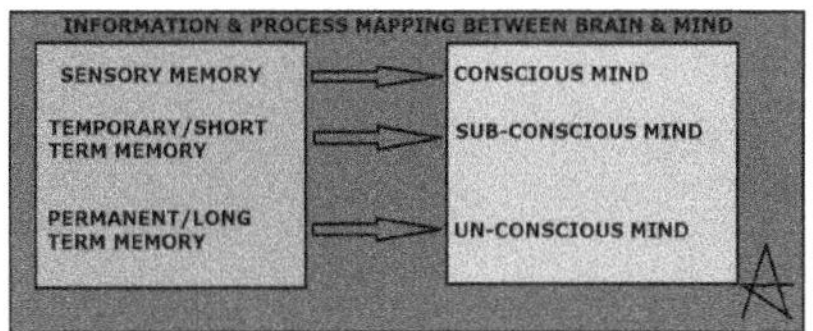

FIG. 2.19:INFORMATION & PROCESS MAPPING BETWEEN BRAIN & MIND

STAGE-7:RECURSIVE TESTING,ANALYSIS & UPDATIONS:

FIG. 2.20:RECURSIVE TESTING,ANALYSIS & UPDATIONS

FIG. 2.21:RECURSIVE TESTING,ANALYSIS & UPDATIONS

FIG. 2.22:RECURSIVE TESTING,ANALYSIS & UPDATIONS

Test yourself recursively(repeatedly).when you study something,study in parts.divide lines of book in small parts that you can process & learn effectively.retrieve information from unconscious mind and if you are able to process a small information,only then proceed for the next information.

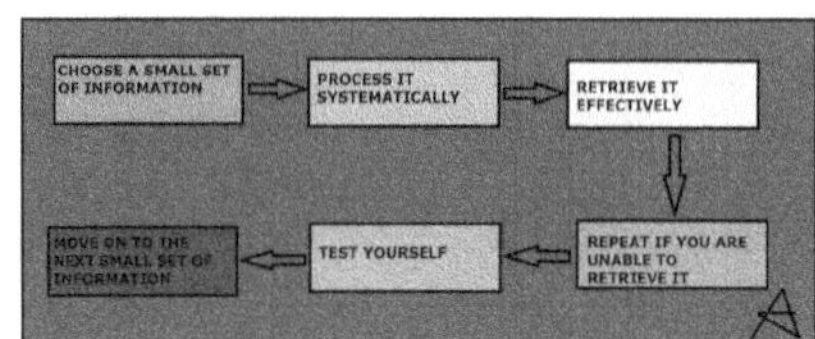

FIG. 2.23:START WORKING WITH A SMALL SET OF INFORMATION

STAGE-8:PRACTICE,ANALYSE AND UPDATE:

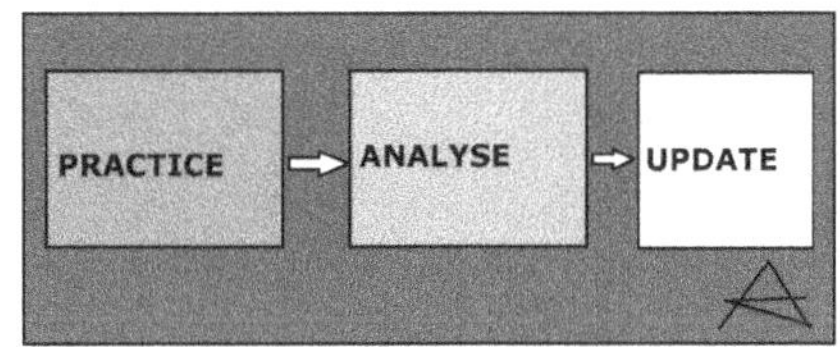

FIG. 2.24:PRACTICE,ANALYSE & UPDATE

Learn the algorithm **gradually**,Have patience,you will feel negative energy and it will demotivate you by creating problems and will try to deviate you from your path.but face problems with a determined mind.

FIG. 2.25:FACE PROBLEMS WITH A DETERMINED MIND

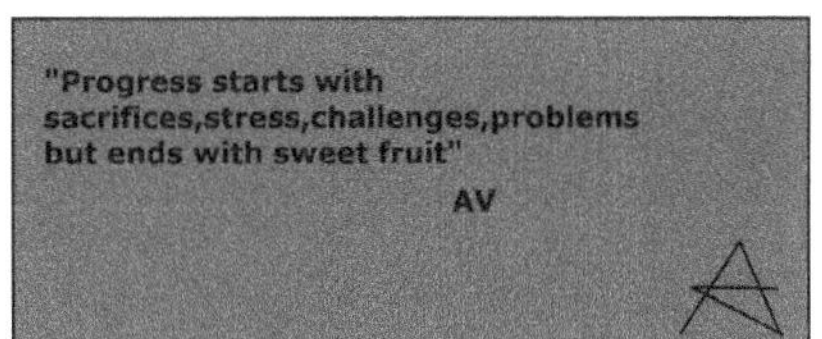

FIG. 2.26:MOTIVATIONAL QUOTE

FIG. 2.27:WORK WITH UNBROKEN FOCUS,YOU WILL BE SUCCESSFUL

work with **unbroken focus**,Let anything to happen but don't get **distracted from your path**.you will be certainly successful a day.

CHAPTER THREE

ENERGY

3.1:INTRODUCTION:

Energy is the fundamental reality of everything.

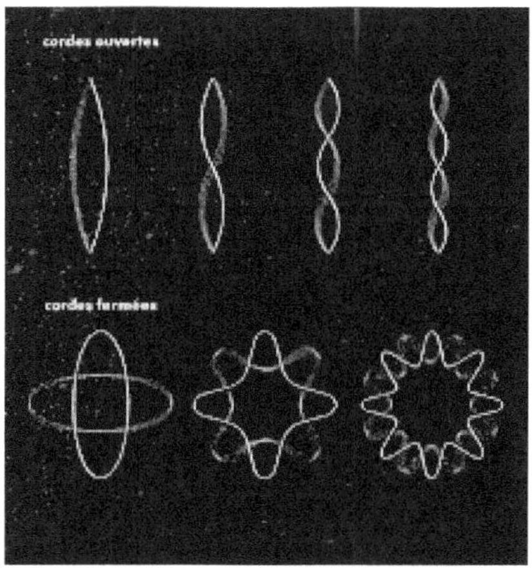

FIG 3.1: ENERGY-THE FUNDAMENTAL REALITY OF EVERYTHING

Entire universe can be seen as a set of strings vibrating with a certain frequency as per the "theory of everything" or "the string theory".

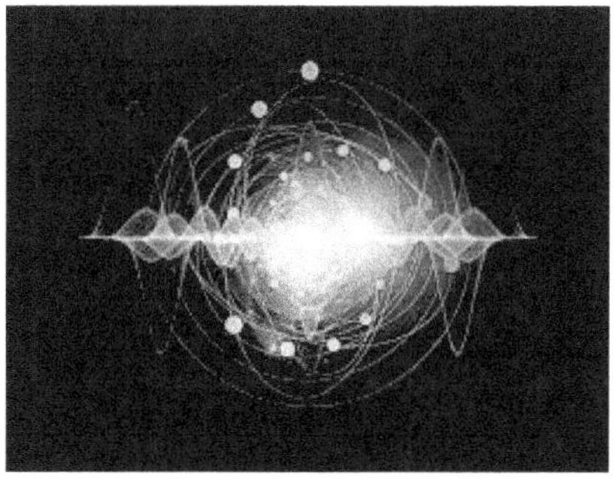

FIG 3.2: UNIVERSE AS A SET OF VIBRATING STRINGS

it's my firm belief that energy in its most basic form is omnipresent with respect to space & time.in hindu mythology that energy is called the **"parbrahma"**.as it is believed that brahma is the creator so parbrahma means something which is before brahma or which creates brahma or which **creates** the creator.

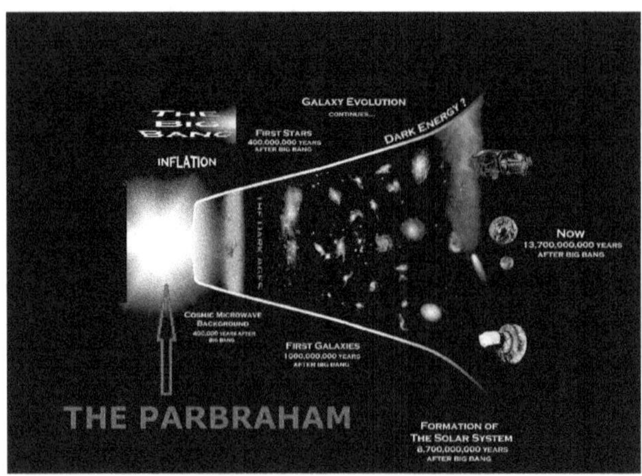

FIG 3.3: THE PARBRAHAM AS PER THEORIES OF HINDUISM

let's start with an experiment.observe your inner world with patience.you can feel 3 types of feelings/emotions/energy within you.

1.The constuctive or positive feelings/emotions/energy:it involves feelings like excitement,enthusiasm,hurry,joy etc.

FIG 3.4: CONSTRUCTIVE OR POSITIVE FEELINGS/EMOTIONS/ENERGY

2.The destructive/negative feelings/emotions/energy:it involves feelings like fear,anxiety,depression,restlessness etc.

FIG 3.5: DISTRUCTIVE OR NEGATIVE FEELINGS/EMOTIONS/ENERGY

3.The observational/neutral feelings:it involves no feelings/emotions.

FIG. 3.6: THE OBSERVATIONAL/NEUTRAL FEELINGS/EMOTIONS/ENERGY

Most of the students start working during positive or negative feelings.but for peak performance you should start with neutral feelings.

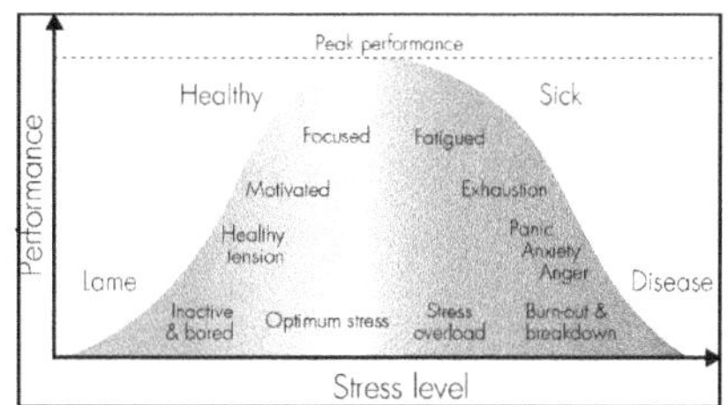

FIG. 3.7: PERFORMANCE VERSUS STRESS GRAPH

1.if you start with positive feeling.you will have a very good start,but soon your energy will be dissipated before reaching the peak performance level.so you have to create more positive energy which will affect your **"MIND-BRAIN SYSTEM"** & you will be overstressed.If it happens then your performance will start to decline.and you will be unable to achieve peak results.

FIG. 3.8: HOW A STUDENT WITH POSITIVE EMOTIONS/ENERGY STARTS A WORK

2.if you start with negative feeling.you will have a very bad start,negative emotions will disturb your"MIND-BRAIN SYSTEM" and your brain will try to put you in a **"FLIGHT MODE"**.you will feel negative emotions like fear,anger,anxiety,depression,restelness etc. soon.you will be unable to focus and will be unable to achieve peak performance.

FIG. 3.9: HOW A STUDENT WITH NEGATIVE EMOTIONS/ENERGY STARTS A WORK

3.if you start with neutral feeling.you will have a gradual start,your "MIND-BRAIN SYSTEM"will have time to adapt to the stress and you will have a self controlled "MIND-BRAIN SYSTEM".you will be able to focus and will achieve peak performance and will decode the frequency at which your "MIND-BRAIN SYSTEM"achieve peak performance.

FIG. 3.10: HOW A STUDENT WITH NEUTRAL EMOTIONS/ENERGY STARTS A WORK

3.2 ORDERED AND SYSTEMATIC "MIND-BRAIN SYSTEM":
Generally students have distractive/unstable thoughts.Due to which they are unable to focus.

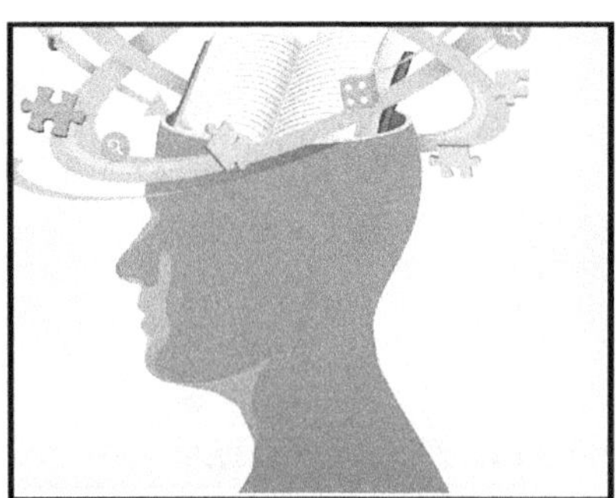

FIG. 3.11: DISTRACTIVE/UNSTABLE THOUGHTS

So lets have have an ordered and systematic **"MIND-BRAIN SYSTEM"**.

FIG. 3.12: ORDERED & SYSTEMATIC "MIND-BRAIN SYSTEM"

FIG. 3.13: ORDERED & SYSTEMATIC "MIND-BRAIN SYSTEM"

3.3: KUNDALINI SHAKTI ACTIVATION:

FIG. 3.14: KUNDALINI SHAKTI ACTIVATION

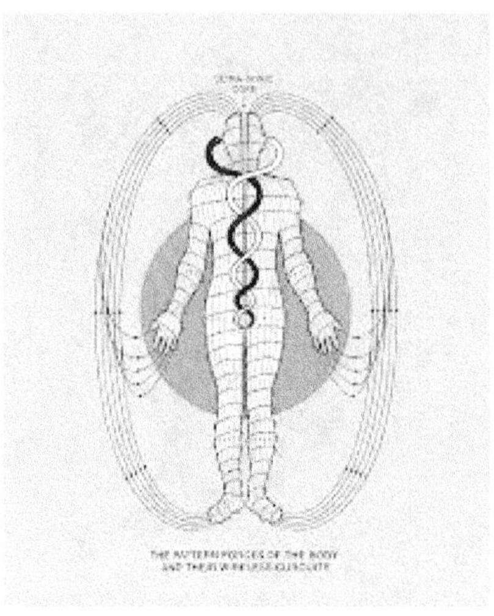

FIG. 3.15: KUNDALINI SHAKTI ACTIVATION

human body is blessed with **kundalini shakti** so that they can have **access to higher dimensions of life** which are beyond **existence,survival and reproduction.**This shakti in inactive form is called **kundalini shakti.**

kundalini resides in inactive form at muladhar/root chakra.but it can be raised from this **chakra tohigher chakras.**Kundalini shakti stablises and strengthen the **"MIND-BRAIN SYSTEM"** for **optimal performance.**

for details on kundalini shakti you can go through my book

"WHO AM I-BY ACHARYA VISHVENDRA",CHAPTER-3:KUNDALINI SHAKTI to learn the process of kundalini shakti activation.

This book can be online purchased from amazon,flipcart and notion press by searching the title **"WHO AM I-BY ACHARYA VISHVENDRA"**

3.4:BEFORE & AFTER KUNDALINI SHAKTI ACIVATION:

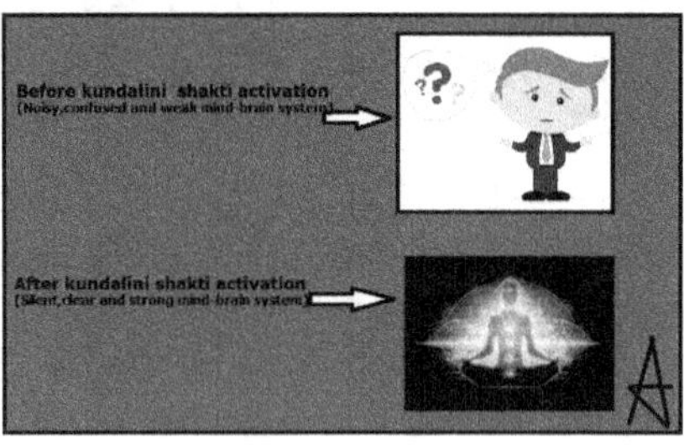

FIG. 3.16: Before & after kundalini Energy Activation

hence we can say that kundalini shakti activation leads to a silent & powerful **"MIND-BRAIN SYSTEM"**

CHAPTER FOUR

PROCESS

After discussing energy, the second dimension is the **processes** used in **cracking competitive exam.**

the **processes** are:

1.Mind conditioning:

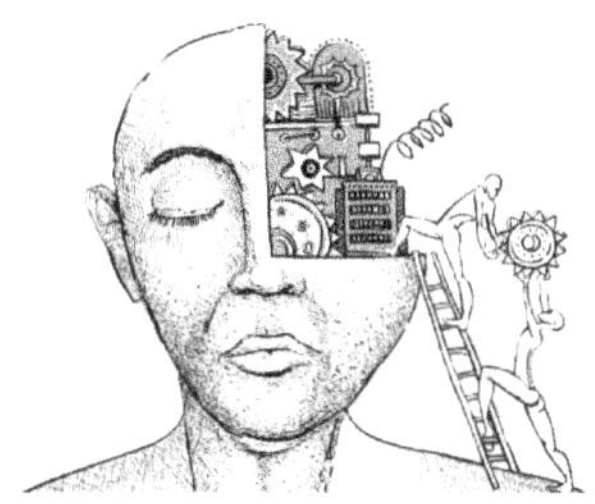

FIG. 4.1: MIND CONDITIONING

Generally our **"MIND-BRAIN SYSTEM"** is busy in reacting on thoughts,so the first process for cracking competitive exam is to make our **"MIND-BRAIN SYSTEM"** thoughtless which is possible by mind condtioning.

"MIND-CONDITIONING" ensures that we actually work on our targets rather than reacting to thoughts.

2.FOCUS ON INPUT INFORMATION:

FIG. 4.2: FOCUS ON INPUT INFORMATION

The next step is to **focus on present.**For checking your focus use **multiple senses** to make sure that you are **able to focus.**For example if you are reading a book.then

(a).first of all scc it from your **right cyc and thcn lcft cyc**

(b).Speak it,listen it first from your **right ear and then left ear**

initially you will have to struggle to keep you focused.however after a certain time you will be able to focus naturally.

3.INFORMATION MAPPING:

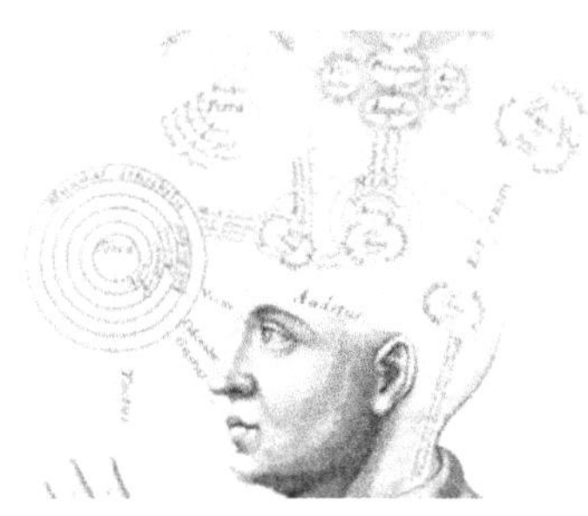

FIG 4.3: INFORMATION MAPPING

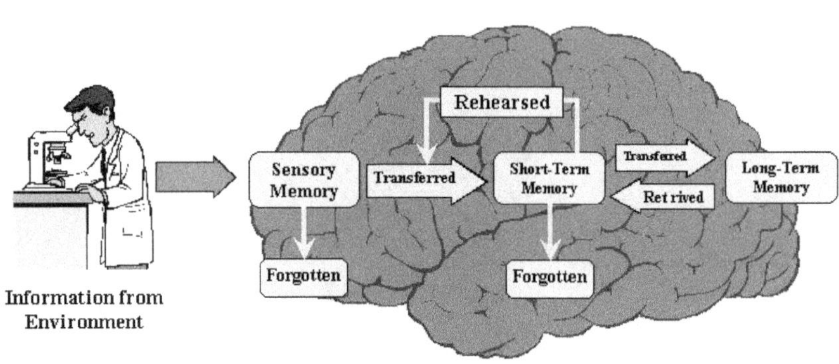

FIG 4.4: INFORMATION MAPPING

Mapping of information from sensory to temporary to permanent memory(conscious to subconscious to unconscious mind):

when we start studying,information is transferred to our **sensory memory** but it is very limited and has to be **transferred to temporary or short term memory.**

Short term memory is also limited and information present in it gets lost after some time and information present in short term memory gets lost after some time.it has to be **transferred to long term or permanent memory.**

FIG 4.5: STUDYING IS PAINFUL BECAUSE OF COMPLEX INFORMATION TRANSFER PROCESS

This process is very complicated and often painful.thats why studying is a painful process.and most of the students are not able to bear the brunt of this painful experience and gets emotionally disturbed while studying.

But this process is central to the process of cracking the competitive exam.you have to bear this painful experience if you want to crack the competitive exam.

generally students are unable to transfer information to permanent memory,they gets distracted and their "MIND-BRAIN SYSTEM" tends to put them in comfortable zone by activating flight mode. you feel comfortable but information mapping is hindered.

As an impact information resides in short term memory which gets lost after sometime.

Because of this students are unable to recall the desired information when they appear for the exam leading to being unsuccessful in the exam.

FIG 4.6: A STUDENT IS UNABLE TO RETRIEE INFORMATION WHEN HE APPEAR FOR A TEST

Hence if you want to perform well in exam,you have to bear the pain of information transfer from sensory to permanent memory.

4.INFORMATION BACKTRACKING:

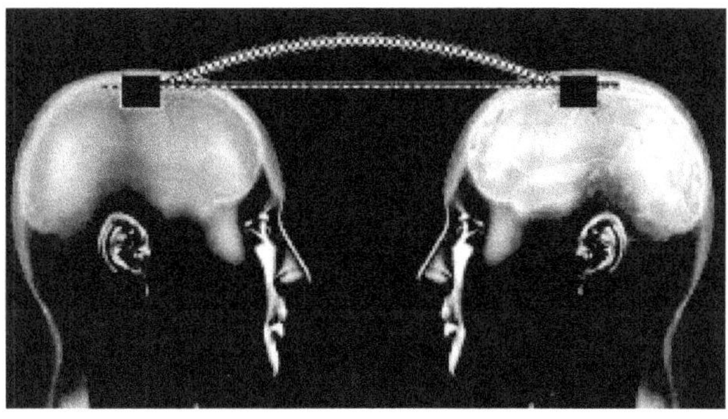

FIG 4.4: INFORMATION BACKTRACKING

Backtracking of information from permanent memory to temporary memory to sensory memory(unconsious to subconscious to conscious mind)

5.INFORMATION UPDATION IF NECESSARY:

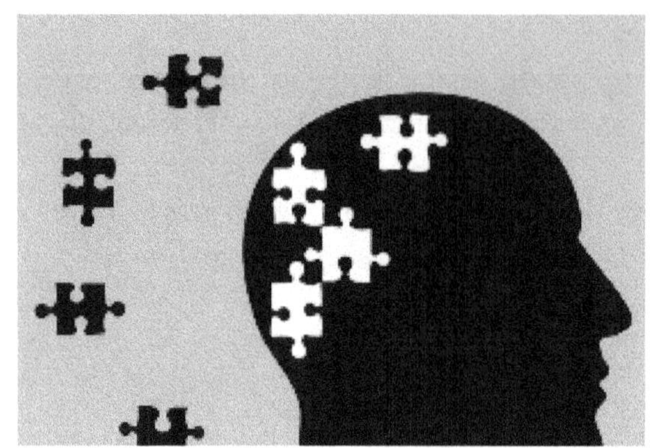

FIG 4.5: INFORMATION UPDATION

6.PRACTICE OF STEP 1-5:

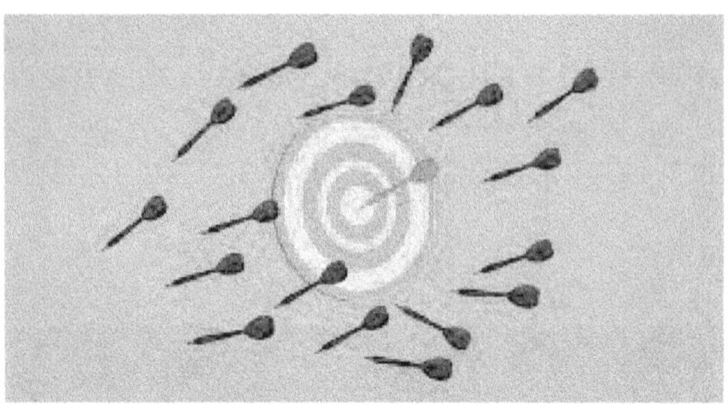

FIG 4.6: PRACTICE

CHAPTER FIVE

INFORMATION

5.1:INTRODUCTION:

FIG.5.1: INFORMATION

The next dimension for cracking a competitive exam is **information.**Any competitive exam has a certain syllabu.syllabus

5.2:TYPES OF INFORMATION:

1.Fundamental or factual information:

Quantity	Symbol	Value	Units
speed of light in vacuo	c	3.00×10^{8}	$m\,s^{-1}$
permeability of free space	μ_0	$4\pi \times 10^{-7}$	$H\,m^{-1}$
permittivity of free space	ε_0	8.85×10^{-12}	$F\,m^{-1}$
magnitude of the charge of electron	e	1.60×10^{-19}	C
the Planck constant	h	6.63×10^{-34}	J s
gravitational constant	G	6.67×10^{-11}	$N\,m^2\,kg^{-2}$
the Avogadro constant	N_A	6.02×10^{23}	mol^{-1}
molar gas constant	R	8.31	$J\,K^{-1}\,mol^{-1}$
the Boltzmann constant	k	1.38×10^{-23}	$J\,K^{-1}$
the Stefan constant	σ	5.67×10^{-8}	$W\,m^{-2}\,K^{-4}$
the Wien constant	α	2.90×10^{-3}	m K
electron rest mass (equivalent to 5.5×10^{-4} u)	m_e	9.11×10^{-31}	kg

FIG.5.2: FUNDAMENTAL OR FACTUAL INFORMATION

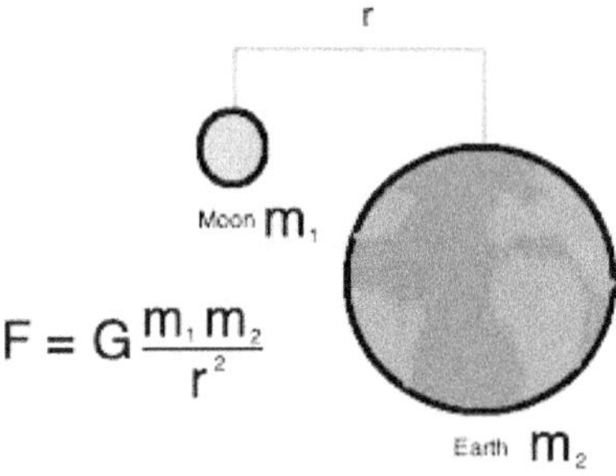

FIG.5.3: FUNDAMENTAL OR FACTUAL INFORMATION

This type of information has to be learnt as a fact using **memorisation techniques/rote mehod** by repeating it **again & again.**

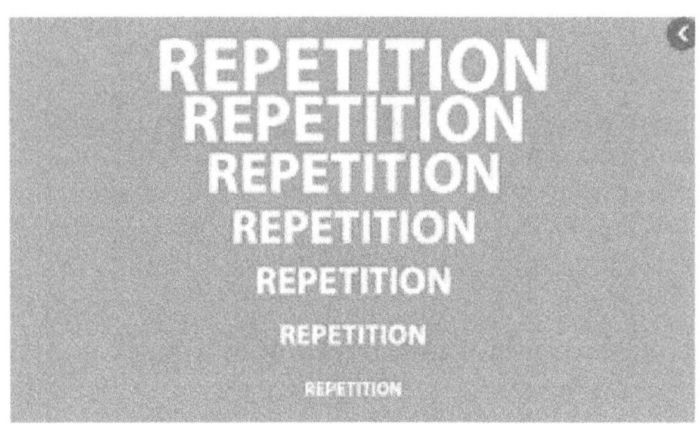

FIG.5.4: REPITITION IS THE KEY TO MASTER FACTUAL INFORMATION

for example value of g,G,law of gravitation,value of c,etc are some facts.you cant create them by calculations or thinking.They have to be memorised. v

2.Derived or mind map based: This type of information requires **memorisation,analysis & multidimensional processing.**

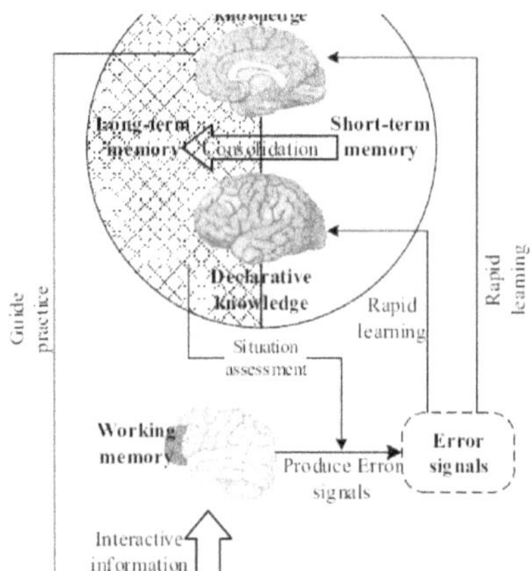

FIG.5.5: MULTIDIMENSIONAL PROCESSING IS REQUIRED FOR DERIVED INFORMATION

For example the electric field inside a sphere is a set of different fundamental informations which requires multistep processing. To learn this information simple memorisation will not work.

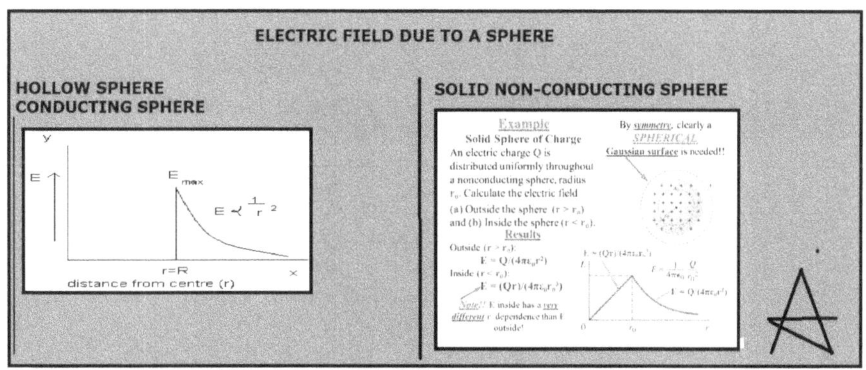

FIG.5.6: MIND MAP BASED INFORMATION

we have to use multistep information processing to transfer this derived information from **sensory memory to permanent memory.**

first of all you have to **analyse the different cases** and need to use your frontal lobe**(responsible for analysis).**

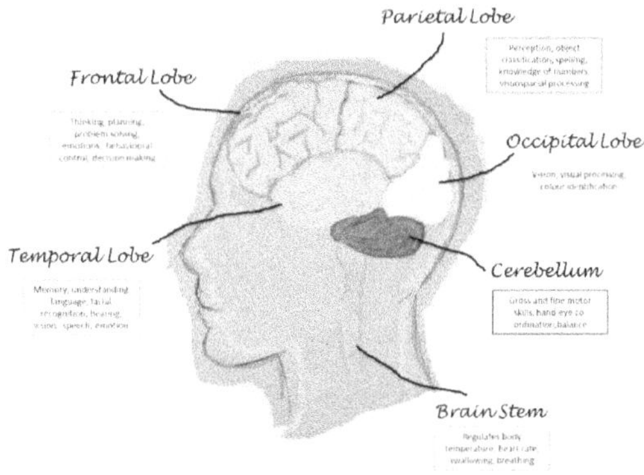

FIG.5.7: BRAIN LOBES & THEIR FUNCTIONS

you have to create mind maps for different cases and then connect them by a link.then you have to repeat this mind-map again and again.

initially you will face difficulty while processing multistep information,but with sufficient practice with patience and strong will power you will be able to learn multistep processing or mind-map processing.

FIG.5.8: HAVE PATIENCE FOR PROCESSING MULTISTEP PROCESSING

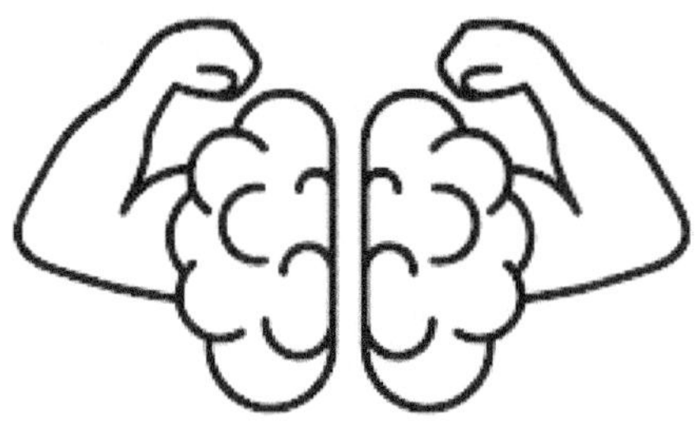

FIG.5.9: HAVE A STRONG WILL POWER FOR PROCESSING MULTISTEP PROCESSING

5.3: INFORMATION ATTRIBUTES:

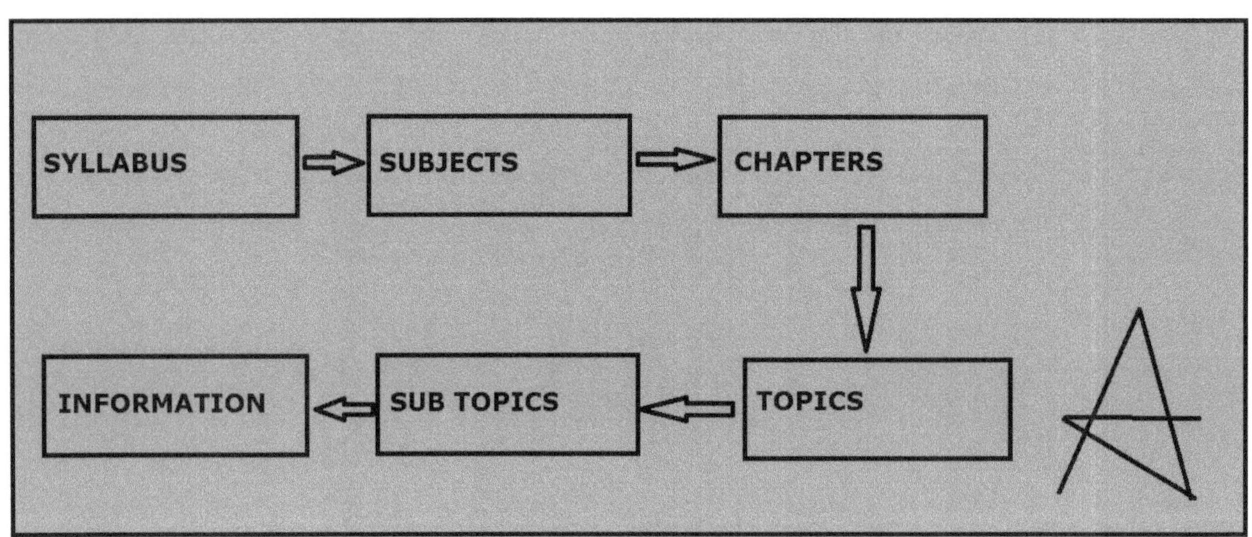

Enter Caption

Develop **information base** which is:

1.concise(minimum relevant information)

2.comprehensive(covers each & every point of syllabus)

3.In a question answer format or mind map formats(so that you can easily grasp it and retrieve it from your unconscious mind as and when needed)

you can refer to my book "**OPTIMAL PHYSICS**" for such a information base,if you are preparing for (**JEE,NEET,ICRA,JET,NDA**).

It can be purchased online At amazon and flipcart.below is a snapshot from amazon.in to help you.

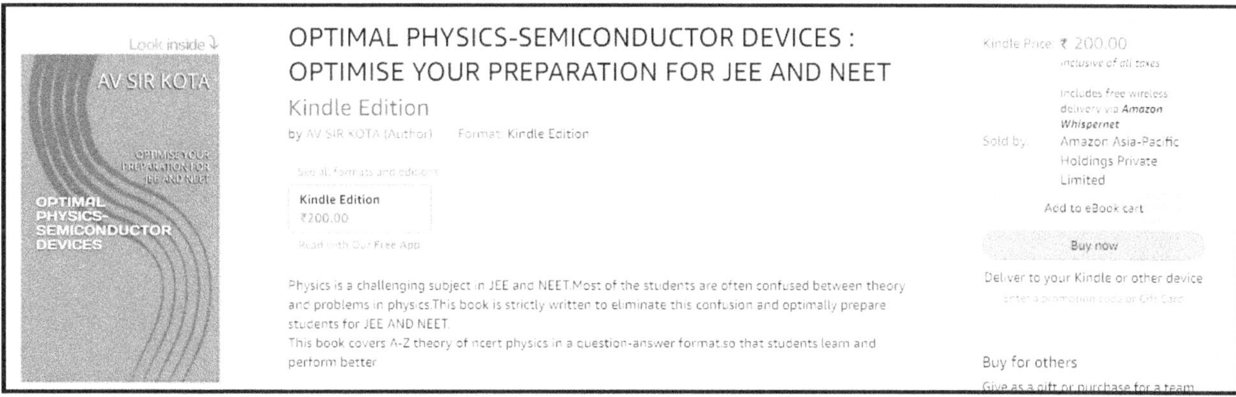

Enter Caption

OUTPUT

6.1.INTRODUCTION:

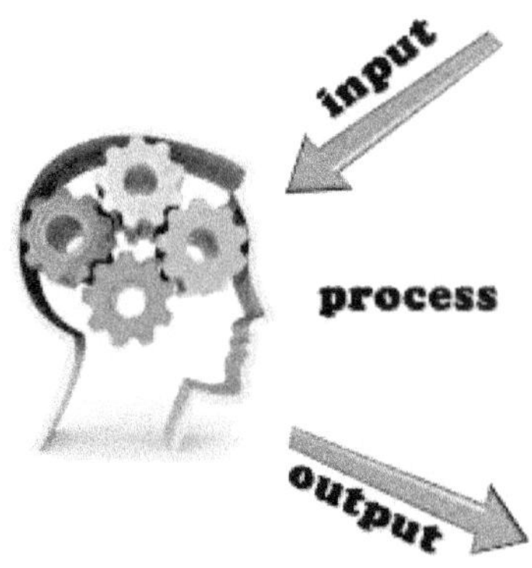

FIG. 6.1:INPUT,PROCESS & OUTPUT

The final outcome of the combination of information,process and energy is the **"OUTPUT"/PERFORMANCE"**.if you can produce **"OUTPUT"/PERFORMANCE"**.you can get anything in **materialistic & non materialistic dimensions of life.**

FIG. 6.2: PERFORMANCE LEADS TO SUCCESS

FIG. 6.3: INTEGRATED OUTPUTS LEADS TO PERFORMANCE

6.2.OUTPUT FOR A STUDENT:

for a student preparing for competitve exam the output is **answer** of question and its proper **marking in the answer sheet**

FIG 6.4:OUTPUT FOR A STUDENT IS FINDING ANSWERS OF A QUESTION

FIG 6.5: OUTPUT FOR A STUDENT IS MAKING ANSWER IN ANSWER SHEET

6.3.OUTPUT & SUCCESS:

Integrated output leads to performance & performance leads to success.

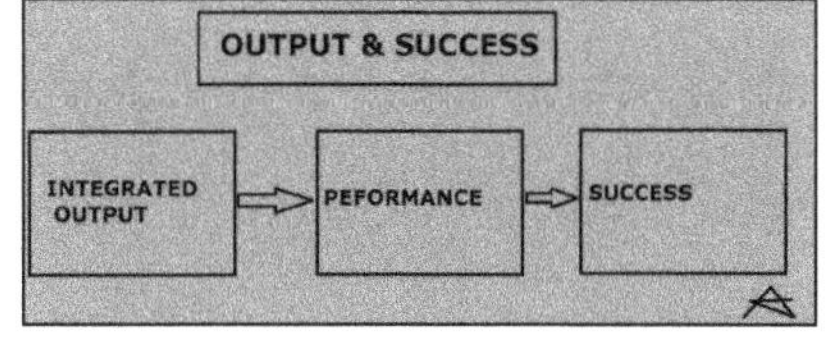

FIG 6.6: INTEGRATED OUTPUT,PERFORMANCE & SUCCESS

FIG 6.7: SUCCESS

FIG 6.8: SUCCESS

FIG 6.9: SUCCESS

CHAPTER SEVEN

PROBLEMS

7.1:INTRODUCTION:

No achievement is done without problems.life when observed beyond existence is a problem itself.so problems are fundamental to human existence.

FIG. 7.1: PROBLEMS

7.2: PROBLEMS FOR A STUDENT:

when you will start preparing for your exam.you will have to face some **problems** like:

1. UNSTABLE THOUGHTS:

when students starts studying the first problem which they face is unstable thoughts.Their mind will try to get attached to **unstable thoughts** which will create a **chain of thoughts** and students will be **trapped in thoughts** and will not be able to study.

FIG. 7.2: UNSTABLE THOUGHTS

2.NEGATIVE EMOTIONS:

The next problem which students will face is negative emotions.They will feel anxiety,sadness,hurry,doubt & ultimately they will stop studying and will run away.as we have 3 types of memories-the sensory memory,the temporary memory & the permanent memory.

generally students are working spontaneously with sensory & temporary memory and a little of permanent memory.but when they study,the purpose is to transfer the information written in book to permanent memory.which is a complex process.

its a painful process as universe tends towards randomness.so developing a system is initiated by resistance from the analytical brain which will tend to keep you in a safe zone.and will initiate flight mode.

such students can boast big to other students & teachers.they create a defence mechanism to prove to others that they are very smart & intelligent.they will create some issue that can explain that they are unable to store information in their permanent memory.they will say that they can think and there is no need to store information.

but deep inside them,something know that they are in a flight mode.thinking is just an elemental part in the whole process of trnsferring information form sensory to permanent memory.different neurons when trying to interconnect generates the feeling of thinking.but its just a spectrum & not the entire process.

in fact thinking is the first step when you try to transfer information from sensory to permanent memory.when some information reaches your sensory memory,it will try to get connect to temporary memory and questions like why?how etc will arise in you.

Its a very elemental process.you will have to work continuously to know the answers to why and how.but this is a very complex process.so students smartly use it as a defence mechanism to cope up with their inability to transfer information from sensory to temporary memory.

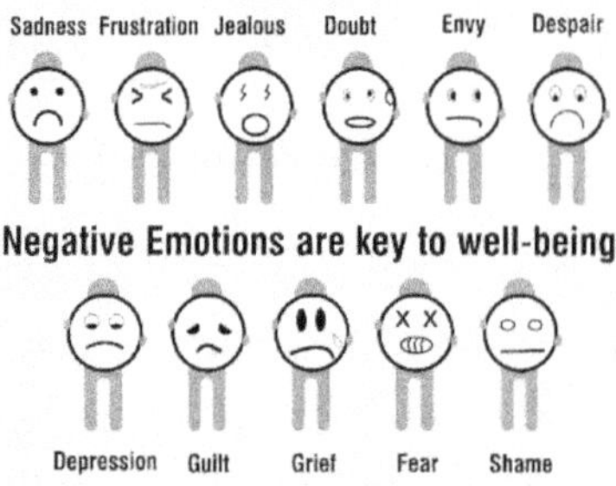

FIG. 7.3: UNSTABLE THOUGHTS

3. WEAK CONCENTRATION POWER:

Because of the complex mental processes that a student will face when he will study,his analytical brain will activate the flight mode to keep him in safe zone.due to which he will loose concentration.he will find some excuse to avoid transfer of information from sensory to permanent memory.

FIG. 7.4: WEAK CONCENTRATION POWER

4. WEAK MEMORY POWER:

due to weak concentration power students are unable to transfer information from sensory to permanent memory which is reflected in the fact that they have a weak memory.

FIG. 7.5: WEAK MEMORY POWER

5. WEAK ANALYSIS POWER:

due to weak concentration and memory students will have weak anaysis power.they will be unable to analyse question and find its answer.

FIG. 7.6: WEAK ANALYSIS POWER

6. WEAK PROBLEM SOLVING SKILLS:

Generally students are unable to solve problems efficiently beacuse of weak memory,concentration and analysis power.They gets frustrated,anxious,angry while solving problems/questions and escape from the process of problem solving.

FIG. 7.7: WEAK PROBLEM SOLVING SKILLS OF STUDENTS

7.WEAK OPTIMAL PERFORMANCE SKILLS:

FIG. 7.8: WEAK OPTIMAL PERFORMANCE SKILLS

Generally students are unable to undergo optimal performance.They work more but get less.There are 3 dimensions of concern-information,process & emotions/energy.These 3 dimensions are mutually exclusive & have to be independently managed for **optimal performance**.but students face problems while giving test.

Lets discuss how to deal with these problems in next chapter

CHAPTER EIGHT

HOW TO DEAL WITH PROBLEMS

8.1:INTRODUCTION:

Life is a **continuos & dynamic process.**if you are a good observer you will know that every second there are problems & issues in life.problems are a natural part of life.so when you face problems that means you have started observing life.so lets discuss about how to deal with problems

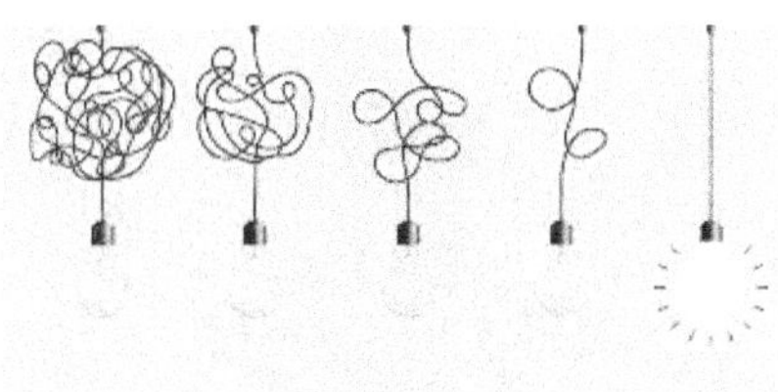

FIG.8.1: FINDING SOLUTIONS OF PROBLEMS

Problems can be solved by facing them with a **silent & powerful mind-brain system.**lets discuss each complexity & its dealing strategies in details.

8.2 DEALING STRATEGY FOR PROBLEMS:

1. DEALING STRATEGY FOR UNSTABLE THOUGHTS: Thoughts are not reality.they are illusions created by the combined impact of information,process & energy.

every time our **"MIND-BRAIN SYSTEM"** is processing information.This processing creates a chain of thoughts,we react to them and are trapped.So the coping mechanism to deal with unstable thoughts is just observe them **without reacting.**

FIG.8.2: OBSERVE UNSTABLE THOUGHTS WITH A SILENT MIND

2.DEALING STRATEGY FOR NEGATIVE EMOTIONS:

create positive emotions to deal with negative emotion.if you are afraid feel the fear and face it.when you will face the negative emotion,it will gradually vanish.

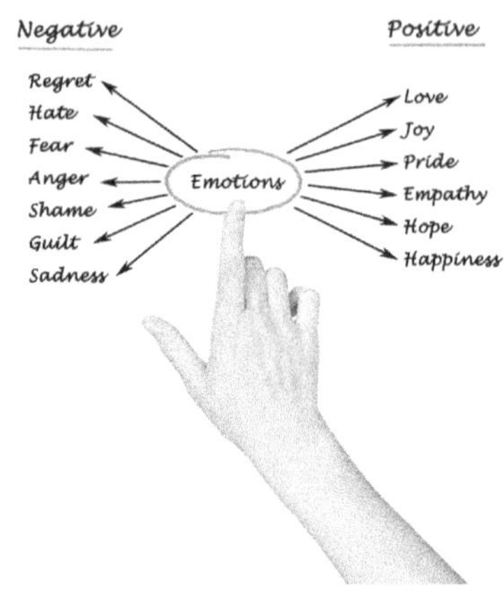

FIG.8.3: NEGATIVE EMOTIONS

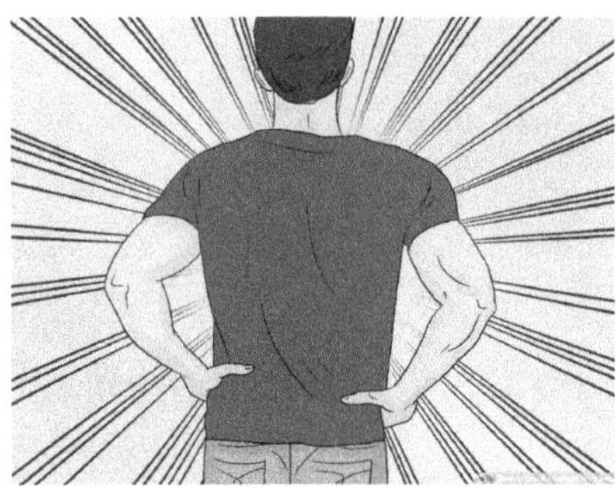

FIG.8.4: FACE NEGATIVE EMOTIONS WITH A SILENT MIND

3.DEALING STRATEGY FOR WEAK CONCENTRATION POWER:

Increase your concentration power by using concentration yantras.they can be online purchased from amazon & flipcart.

you can also refer to the book **"DEVELOPING MIND,DEVELOP INDIA-OST"** for learning techniques for having deep concentration power.it's can be online purchased from amazon,flipcart & notion press.

FIG.8.5: USE CONCENTRATION YANTRA FOR SHARP MEMORY

FIG.8.6: USE "DEVELOPING MIND-DEVELOP INDIA(OST)"FOR DEEP CONCENTRATION POWER

4. DEALING STRATEGY FOR WEAK MEMORY POWER:

You can have a sharp memory by suitable **"MIND-TRAINING PROGRAMS"**.

you can also refer to the book **"DEVELOPING MIND,DEVELOP INDIA-OST"** for learning techniques for having deep concentration power.it can be online purchased from amazon,flipcart & notion press.

FIG.8.7: DEVELOP SHARP MEMORY

5. DEALING STRATEGY FOR WEAK ANALYSIS POWER:

Develop sharp analysis power.you can also refer to the book **"DEVELOPING MIND,DEVELOP INDIA-OST"** for learning techniques for having sharp analysis power.it can be online purchased from amazon,flipcart & notion press.

FIG.8.8: DEVELOP SHARP ANALYSIS POWER

6. DEALING STRATEGY FOR WEAK PROBLEM SOLVING SKILLS:

Develop sharp problem solving skills.you can also refer to the book "**DEVELOPING MIND,DEVELOP INDIA-OST**" for learning techniques of sharp problem solving skills.it can be online purchased from amazon,flipcart & notion press.

FIG.8.9: DEVELOP SHARP PROBLEM SOLVING SKILLS

These are some of the dealing strategies for dealing with problems concerned with a student while he prepares for competitive exams.

hence you must face the problems,prepare yourself mentally and get successful in cracking the competitive exam.

Most of the students fails in competitive exams because they are unable to face the problems which arises during their preparation.hence if you aspire to crack a competitive exam then you must face the problems and learn to resolve them.

CHAPTER NINE

OPTIMAL PERFORMANCE

9.1:INTRODUCTION:

Performance is the key to success & optimal performance is the key to optimal success.

FIG.9.1: OPTIMAL PERFORMANCE

9.2:WHY OPTIMAL PERFORMANCE?

somebody has well said that **"work speaks better than word"**.

Generally students are unable to optimally use their body,brain,mind,energy & time to achieve optimal performance.As performance is the only deciding factor in life so the entire strategy should be performance oriented.

In our education system the focus is on information & its rote learning.but no training is explicitly given about the process and the mental powers to achieve optimal performance.

only a few exceptional sudents who are self motivated are able to learn the process and mental powers to achieve optimal performance,due to which only a few students succeeds in competitive exams.

where as most of the students just struggle with information,process & emotions/energy and are unable to develop effective information processing skills & other mental powers(strong will power, deep concentration power, power to achieve silent mind, sharp memory power, power of sharp problem solving skills, sharp analytical skill power, sharp optimal performance power). which is the core requirement of today's dynamic world.

you can also refer to the book **"DEVELOPING MIND,DEVELOP INDIA-OST"** for learning techniques for developing mental powers.it can be purchased online from amazon,flipcart & notion press.

9.3:BEYOND CRACKING COMPETITIVE EXAM:

let's extend our discussion beyond cracking competitive exam,because cracking competitive exam is the first step toward career.the final step is a decent job.As per media reports 80 percent youth are not employable.

FIG.9.2: 80% INDIAN YOUNGSTERS NOT TRAINED FOR ANY JOB

source:(https://www.marketingmind.in/80-indian-youngsters-not-trained-job-says-infosys-co-founder-narayana-murthy/)

so optimal performance is not just limited to cracking competiitve exam but its also necessary to get a decent job.

9.4: YERKES-DODSON THEORY:

Yerkes-Dodson theory relates stress & performance.

It states that optimal performance occurs at mediocre stress.Too little or too much stress results in relatively poor performance.

The theory has been around since 1908, when psychologists Robert Yerkes and John Dillingham Dodson performed experiments on mouse and came to decode the graph as shown in the figure.

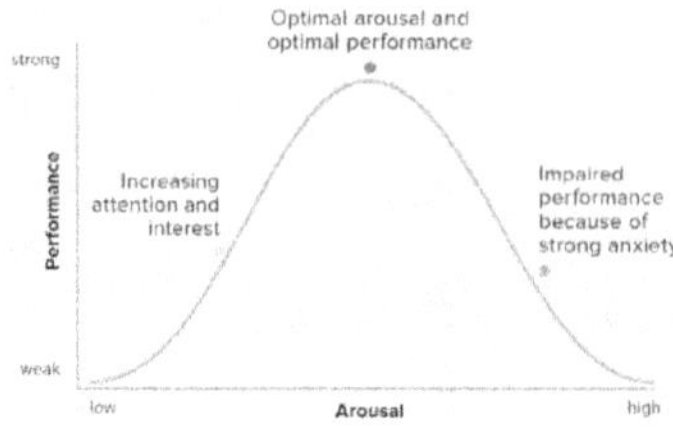

FIG.9.3: YERKES-DODSON GRAPH

The Yerkes-Dodson graph is an U-shaped graph.initially at low stress performance is low,at mediocre stress performance is optimal & at high stress performance again decreases. The optimal performance come together in the middle of the curve.

9.5: THEORY OF RESONANCE:

In a series R-L-C circuit current is maximum at resonannt frequency as shown in the below graph.This resonant frequency depends on the capacitance & inductance of the circuit.

in the similar way a human "MIND-BRAIN SYSTEM" is reminiscent of a series R-L-C CIRCUIT,as current flows in a series R-L-C circuit,in the same way neurons flow in the brain.you can see the analogy between graphs.

Resonance frequency is characterised by a thoughtless,suggestionless state of mind in which your performance is at its peak.it can be known only by practice.it takes time to decode your resonant frequency.

So we can interpret it as "Every body has a resonant frequency at which his/her performance is maximum".

you should decode this frequency and operate at this frequency.

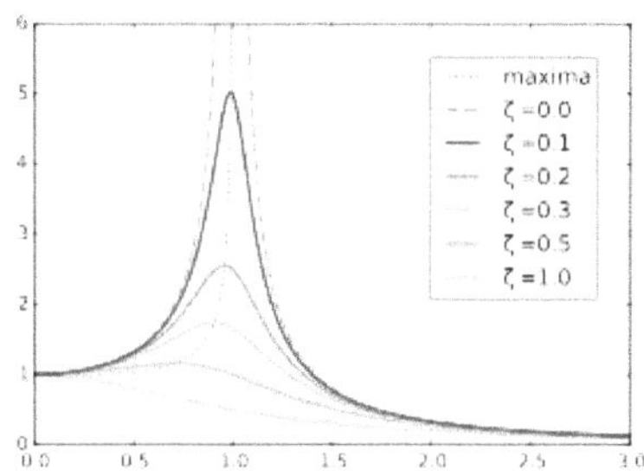

FIG.9.4: RESONANCE IN R-L-C CIRCUIT

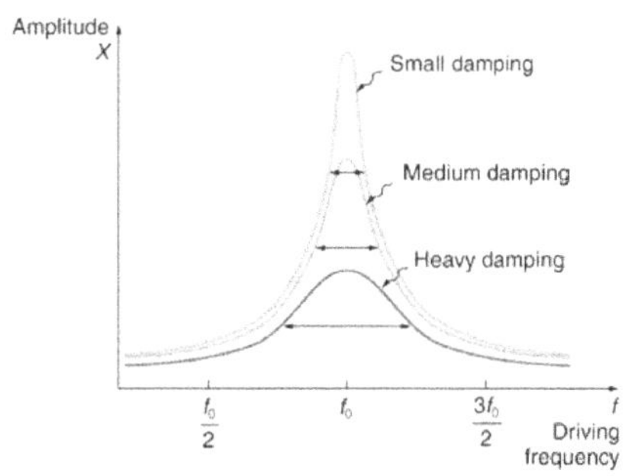

FIG.9.5: RESONANCE IN R-L-C CIRCUIT

$$\frac{1}{\omega_o C} = \omega_o L$$

$$\therefore \ \omega_o = \frac{1}{\sqrt{LC}}$$

$$\text{or} \quad 2\pi\nu_o = \frac{1}{\sqrt{LC}}$$

$\nu_o = \dfrac{1}{2\pi\sqrt{LC}}$ is called resonant frequency

FIG.9.6: RESONANT FREQUENCY

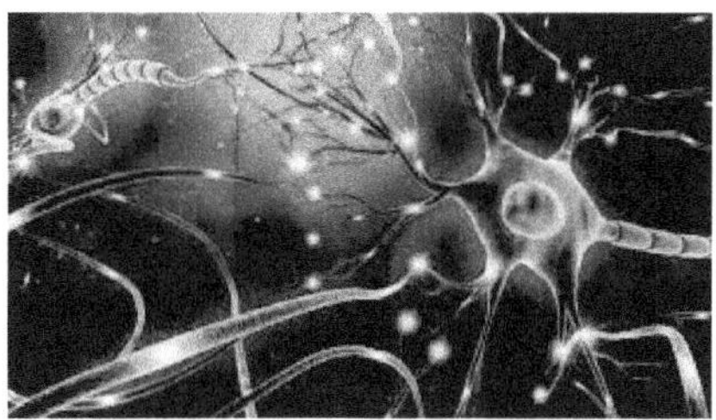

FIG.9.7: NEURONS FLOW IN BRAIN

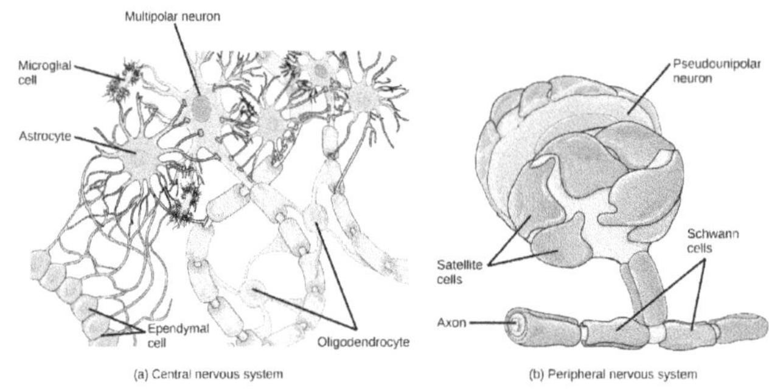

FIG.9.8: NEURONS FLOW IN BRAIN

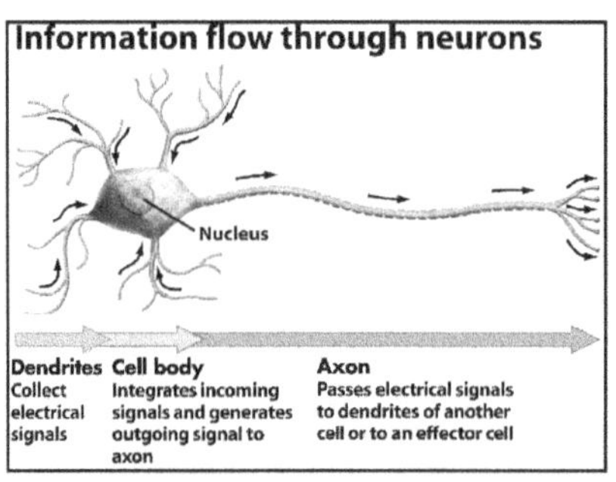

FIG.9.9: INFORMATION FLOW IN NEURONS

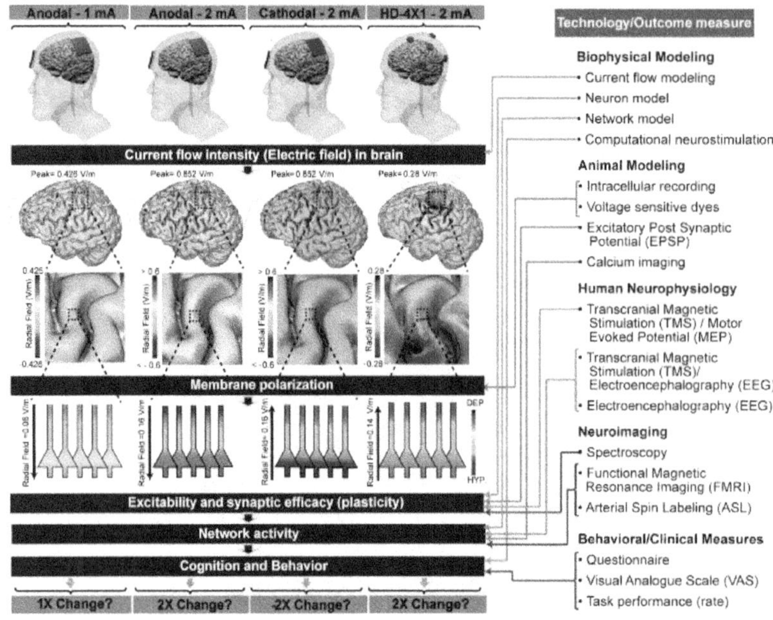

FIG.9.10: NEURAL ACTIVITY AT DIFFERENT CURRENT FLOW INTENSITY

CHAPTER TEN

2 YEAR PLAN

10.1:INTRODUCTION:

FIG. 10.1: 2 YEAR PLAN

Lets start with plannings for "CRACKING THE COMPETITIVE EXAMS".Generally we have 2 year and 1 year plan.lets start with JEE,NEET & CUET 2 years plan.

2 years plan is for students in class 11.

10.2:PLAN FOR CLASS 11:

PHYSICS [P]

S. No.	Topic Name/Sequence	No of Lectures	Starting Date
1	Mathematical Tools	12	09-Apr-18
2	Rectilinear Motion	5	01-May-18
3	Projectile Motion	6	12-May-18
4	Relative Motion	6	22-May-18
5	NLM	10	01-Jun-18
6	Miscellaneous	6	19-Jun-18
7	Friction	5	25-Jun-18
8	Work, Power & Energy (WPE)	10	04-Jul-18
9	Circular Motion	7	23-Jul-18
10	Centre of mass	10	06-Aug-18
11	Rigid Body Dynamics	15	27-Aug-18
12	Simple Harmonic Motion (SHM)	7	24-Sep-18
13	Fluid Mechanics	4	06-Oct-18
14	Miscellaneous	1	11-Oct-18
15	Surface Tension	3	15-Oct-18
16	Unit & Dimension	1	22-Oct-18
17	Measurement & Error	1	23-Oct-18
18	Elasticity & Viscosity	3	24-Oct-18
19	Miscellaneous	3	30-Oct-18
20	String Wave	8	16-Nov-18
21	Sound Waves	7	31-Dec-18
22	Kinetic Theory of Gases & Thermodynamics	7	11-Dec-18
23	Calorimetry & Thermal Expansion	6	24-Dec-18
Total No. of Lectures		**143**	

CHEMISTRY [C]

S. No.	Topic Name/Sequence	No of Lectures	Starting Date
1	Introduction to Chemistry	4	09-Apr-18
2	Atomic Structure	15	23-Apr-18
3	Mole Concept	12	25-Jun-18
4	Gaseous state 1 (Ideal gases)	8	24-Jul-18
5	Chemical Equilibrium	8	13-Aug-18
6	Gaseous state 2 (Real gases)	4	03-Sep-18
7	Thermodynamics	14	11-Sep-18
8	Ionic Equilibrium (Elementary)	7	15-Oct-18
9	Ionic Equilibrium (Advanced)	6	16-Nov-18
10	s-Block Elements	6	01-Dec-18
11	p-Block elements (13-14)	7	17-Dec-18
12	IUPAC Nomenclature	11	09-Apr-18
13	Structural Isomerism	4	05-May-18
14	Structural identification	3	14-May-18
15	Periodic Table	7	22-May-18
16	BIN	4	11-Jun-18
17	All basic concepts of Org. Chem (ABC-I)	6	25-Jun-18
18	ABC-II	3	10-Jul-18
19	Chemical Bonding-I	7	21-Jul-18
20	Chemical Bonding-II	6	06-Aug-18
21	Chemical Bonding-III	5	25-Aug-18
22	Chemical Bonding-IV	4	10-Sep-18
23	Chemical Bonding-V	4	18-Sep-18
24	ABC-III	3	02-Oct-18
25	ABC-IV	3	15-Oct-18
26	GOC-I	10	22-Oct-18
27	GOC-II	12	04-Dec-18
Total No. of Lectures		**183**	

MATHEMATICS [M]

S. No.	Topic Name/Sequence	No of Lectures	Starting Date
1	Fundamentals of Mathematics-I	14	09-Apr-18
2	Quadratic Equation	13	03-May-18
3	Trigonometry	15	26-May-18
4	Sequence & Series	11	25-Jun-18
5	Fundamentals of Mathematics-II	13	14-Jul-18
6	Binomial Theorem	7	06-Aug-18
7	Permutation & Combination	12	20-Aug-18
8	Straight Line	15	10-Sep-18
9	Statistics	2	08-Oct-18
10	Mathematical Induction	2	11-Oct-18
11	Solution of Triangle	7	15-Oct-18
12	Mathematical Reasoning	4	29-Oct-18
13	Circle	12	16-Nov-18
14	Conic Section	16	07-Dec-18
Total No. of Lectures		**143**	

FIG. 10.2: CLASS 11 PLAN

10.3: PLAN FOR CLASS 12:

PHYSICS [P]

S. No.	Topic Name/Sequence	No of Lectures	Starting Date
1	Geometrical Optics	22	16-02-2021
2	Electrostatics	24	05-04-2021
3	Gravitation	5	19-05-2021
4	Current Electricity	12	27-05-2021
5	Heat Transfer	5	21-06-2021
6	Capacitance	10	30-06-2021
7	EMF	14	20-07-2021
8	EMI	11	23-08-2021
9	Alternating Current	5	16-09-2021
10	Measurement Error & Experiments	3	27-09-2021
11	Modern Physics-I	10	30-09-2021
12	Nuclear Physics	6	20-10-2021
13	Wave Optics	7	13-11-2021
14	Semiconductor	6	24-11-2021
15	PQC	2	06-12-2021
16	EMW	2	08-12-2021
Total No. of Lectures		**144**	

CHEMISTRY [C]

S. No.	Topic Name/Sequence	No of Lectures	Starting Date
	PHYSICAL/ INORGANIC		
1	Solution & Colligative Properties	9	15-02-2021
2	Coordination compound	13	09-03-2021
3	Solid State	10	14-04-2021
4	Electrochemistry	13	04-05-2021
5	Metallurgy	6	02-06-2021
6	Qualitative Analysis(anion)	6	16-06-2021
7	p-Block(N & O)	9	30-06-2021
8	Equivalent concept & titrations	6	02-08-2021
9	Halogen & noble gas	5	23-08-2021
10	Chemical Kinetics	10	06-09-2021
11	Surface chemistry	4	28-09-2021
12	Qualitative Analysis (Cation)	5	11-10-2021
13	d & f-Block Element	4	20-10-2021
14	s-Block	4	11-11-2021
15	p-Block (13-14 groups)	5	23-11-2021
	ORGANIC		
1	GOC-II	8	15-02-2021
2	Stereoisomerism	14	09-03-2021
3	ORM-I	12	04-05-2021
4	ORM-II	11	07-06-2021
5	Reduction, Oxidation & Hydrolysis	9	07-07-2021
6	ORM-III	7	02-08-2021
7	ORM-IV	5	23-08-2021
8	Handout	1	07-09-2021
9	Aromatic Compound	6	13-09-2021
10	Carbonyl Compounds, Carboxylic Acid & Acid Derivatives	7	05-10-2021
11	Biomolecules & Polymer	7	11-11-2021
12	Chemistry in Everyday Life	1	06-12-2021
13	Physical Properties, POC-II	1	07-12-2021
Total No. of Lectures		**198**	

MATHEMATICS [M]

S. No.	Topic Name/Sequence	No of Lectures	Starting Date
1	Relation, Functions & ITF	19	15-02-2021
2	Rediscussion of P & C Sheet	1	18-03-2021
3	Probability	11	22-03-2021
4	Limits, Continuity & Derivability	15	19-04-2021
5	Method of Differentiation	4	18-05-2021
6	Rediscussion of Straight Line Sheet	1	25-05-2021
7	Application of Derivatives	17	26-05-2021
8	Rediscussion of circle Sheet	1	28-06-2021
9	Matrices & Determinant	12	29-06-2021
10	Rediscussion of Conic Section Sheet	1	21-07-2021
11	Vector & 3-D	18	22-07-2021
12	Rediscussion of Trigonometry Sheet	1	25-08-2021
13	Indefinite Integration	10	30-08-2021
14	Definite Integratin & Its Application	13	15-09-2021
15	Rediscussion of Quadratic Equation Sheet	1	14-10-2021
16	Differential Equation	8	16-10-2021
17	Linear Programming	2	13-11-2021
18	Binary Operation	1	16-11-2021
19	Complex Number	12	17-11-2021
Total No. of Lectures		**148**	

FIG. 10.3: CLASS 12 PLAN

CHAPTER ELEVEN

1 YEAR PLAN

11.1: INTRODUCTION:

Lets start with plannings for "CRACKING THE COMPETITIVE EXAMS".Generally we have 2 year and 1 year plan.lets start with JEE,NEET & CUET 1 years plan.

1 year plan is for students in class 12.

FIG. 11.1: 1 YEAR PLAN

11.2: 1 YEAR PLAN:

PHYSICS [P]

S. No.	Topic Name/Sequence	No of Lectures	Starting Date
1	Rectilinear motion	5	02-Aug-21
2	Projectile motion	4	10-Aug-21
3	Relative motion	8	17-Aug-21
4	Geometrical Optics	19	30-Aug-21
5	Newton's laws of motion	9	23-Sep-21
6	Friction	4	04-Oct-21
7	Work, Power, Energy	7	08-Oct-21
8	Electrostatics	13	16-Oct-21
9	Gravitation	5	11-Nov-21
10	Current electricity	8	17-Nov-21
11	Capacitance	8	26-Nov-21
12	Circular motion	5	06-Dec-21
13	Centre of mass	7	11-Dec-21
14	Rigid body dynamics	11	20-Dec-21
15	Simple Harmonic motion	8	01-Jan-22
16	String wave	5	08-Jan-22
17	Sound wave	6	14-Jan-22
18	Wave Optics	3	21-Jan-22
19	EM Wave	1	25-Jan-22
20	Semiconductor	3	26-Jan-22
21	POC	2	29-Jan-22
22	EMF	7	01-Feb-22
23	EMI	5	09-Feb-22
24	Alternating Current	3	15-Feb-22
25	Modern Physics-I	5	18-Feb-22
26	Nuclear Physics	4	24-Feb-22
27	Fluid Mechanics	5	01-Mar-22
28	Surface Tension	3	07-Mar-22
29	Elasticity and viscosity	2	10-Mar-22
30	KTG and thermodynamics	7	12-Mar-22
31	Calorimetry & thermal expansion	3	21-Mar-22
32	Heat transfer	3	24-Mar-22
Total No. of Lectures		**186**	

CHEMISTRY [C]

S. No.	Topic Name/Sequence	No of Lectures	Starting Date
	PHYSICAL/ INORGANIC		
1	Mole Concept	6	02-Aug-21
2	Quantum Mech. model of atom	2	23-Aug-21
3	Periodic Table	3	30-Aug-21
4	Real Gases	4	07-Sep-21
5	Chemical Bonding-1	3	15-Sep-21
6	Chemical Bonding-2	3	21-Sep-21
7	Chemical Bonding-3	2	27-Sep-21
8	Chemical Bonding-4	1	29-Sep-21
9	Chemical Bonding-5	4	30-Sep-21
10	Chemical Equilibrium	6	07-Oct-21
11	Ionic Equilibrium (Elementary)	7	19-Oct-21
12	Coordination compounds	9	11-Nov-21
13	Electrochemistry	8	25-Nov-21
14	Metallurgy	3	09-Dec-21
15	Qualitative Analysis-I	4	15-Dec-21
16	p-Block (Halogen & Noble gases)	3	22-Dec-21
17	Chemical Kinetics	8	28-Dec-21
18	Solution & Colligative Properties	8	11-Jan-22
19	Solid State	7	25-Jan-22
20	Surface Chemistry	4	07-Feb-22
21	Qualitative Analysis-II	4	14-Feb-22
22	s-Block	2	21-Feb-22
23	p-Block(N & O)	4	23-Feb-22
24	Thermodynamics & Thermochem.	7	02-Mar-22
25	p-Block Elements (B&C Family)	3	15-Mar-22
26	Equivalent Concept	3	21-Mar-22
27	d-Block Element	2	24-Mar-22
28	Ionic Equilibrium (Advance)	3	29-Mar-22
	ORGANIC		
1	IUPAC Nomenclature	4	02-Aug-21
2	Structural isomerism	1	16-Aug-21
3	Structure Identification & POC-I	2	17-Aug-21
4	Structural Identification & POC	1	24-Aug-21
5	GOC-I	7	30-Aug-21
6	GOC-II	7	20-Sep-21
7	Stereoisomerism (Mains)	5	12-Oct-21
8	ORM-I	5	11-Nov-21
9	ORM-II	8	23-Nov-21
10	Reduction, Oxidation & Hydrolysis	4	13-Dec-21
11	ORM-III	5	21-Dec-21
12	ORM-IV	4	03-Jan-22
13	Aromatic Compound	5	11-Jan-22
14	Hydrocarbon	1	25-Jan-22
15	Carbonyl comp., Acid & derivatives	7	31-Jan-22
16	Biomolecules & Polymers	5	22-Feb-22
17	Stereoisomerism (Advanced)	4	14-Mar-22
18	Physical properties	1	28-Mar-22
19	Chemistry In Everyday Life	1	29-Mar-22
Total No. of Lectures		**210**	

MATHEMATICS [M]

S. No.	Topic Name/Sequence	No of Lectures	Starting Date
1	Fundamentals of Mathematics	17	02-Aug-21
2	Quadratic Equation	8	30-Aug-21
3	Relation, Function & ITF	14	10-Sep-21
4	Statistics	3	27-Sep-21
5	Sequence & Series	7	30-Sep-21
6	Matrices & Determinant	10	06-Oct-21
7	Straight Line	10	20-Oct-21
8	Circle	7	11-Nov-21
9	Limits, Continuity & Derivability	11	19-Nov-21
10	Application of Derivatives	13	06-Dec-21
11	Mathematical Reasoning	3	23-Dec-21
12	Conic Section	12	28-Dec-21
13	Indefinite Integration	6	13-Jan-22
14	Definite Integration & Its App.	11	21-Jan-22
15	Differential Equation	5	03-Feb-22
16	Vector & 3-D	13	09-Feb-22
17	Complex Number	9	24-Feb-22
18	Solution of Triangle	3	07-Mar-22
19	Binomial Theorem	8	10-Mar-22
20	Permutation & Combination	9	17-Mar-22
21	Probability	8	28-Mar-22
Total No. of Lectures		**183**	

FIG. 11.2: 1 YEAR PLAN

CHAPTER TWELVE

LAST MONTH PLAN

12.1:INTRODUCTION:

Let's discuss the plans during the last month.

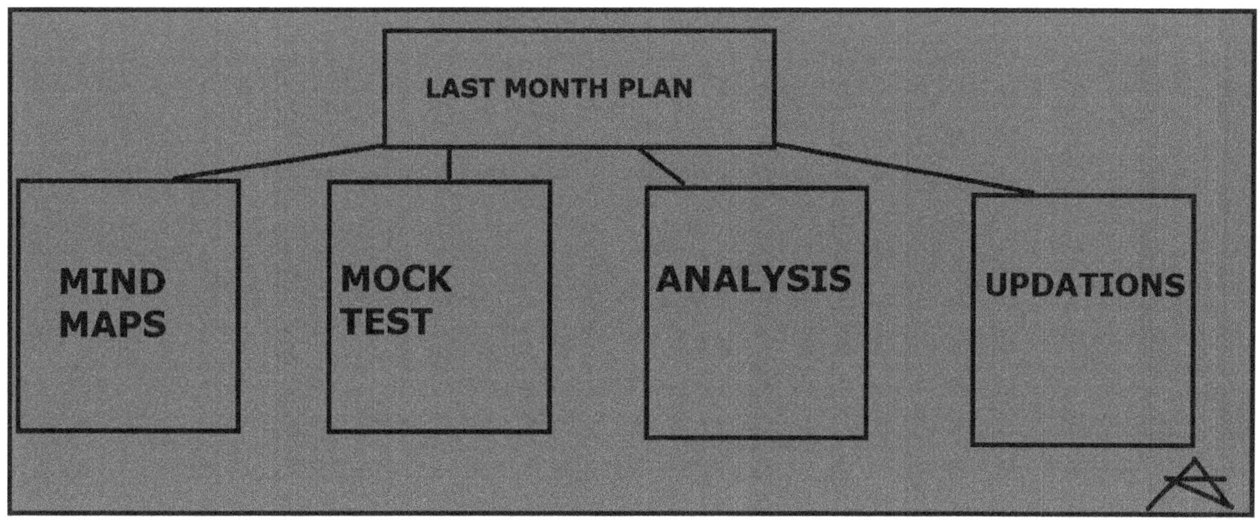

FIG. 12.1:LAST MONTH PLAN

12.2:ASPECTS OF CONCERN: during last month we have 4 aspects of concern-

1.MIND MAPS:

Mind maps ensures interconnected information which is easy to retrieve.so every point of syllabus should be transformed in the form of "**MIND MAPS**" before the last month.

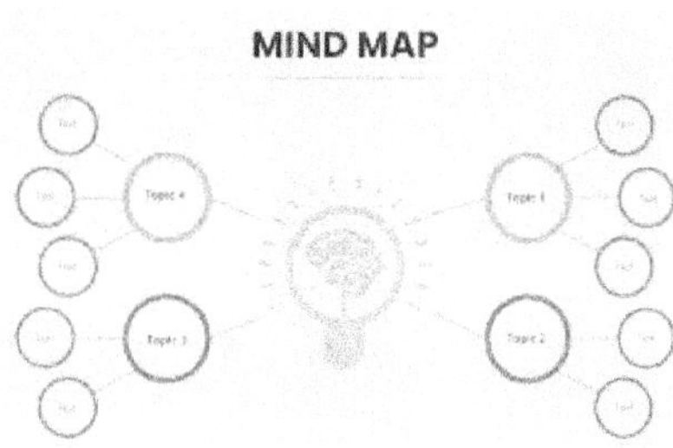

FIG. 12.2: MIND MAPS

2.MOCK TEST:

Last month should be used for daily mock test so that students becomes mentally adaptive to the test environment.it is observed that most of the students fails in competitive exams because they are not mentally comfortable with the testing environment.

hence mock tests are crucial for mental compatibility with the exam.

FIG. 12.3: MOCK TEST

3.ANALYSIS:

Analysis of your progress is essential for improvement.analyse your mock test results.make a list of your mistakes and rectify them.

FIG. 12.4: ANALYSIS

4.UPDATIONS:

Update your strategies so that you can perform better next time.

FIG. 12.5: UPDATIONS

CHAPTER THIRTEEN

LAST WEEK PLAN

13.1:INTRODUCTION:

Let's discuss the the last week plan.

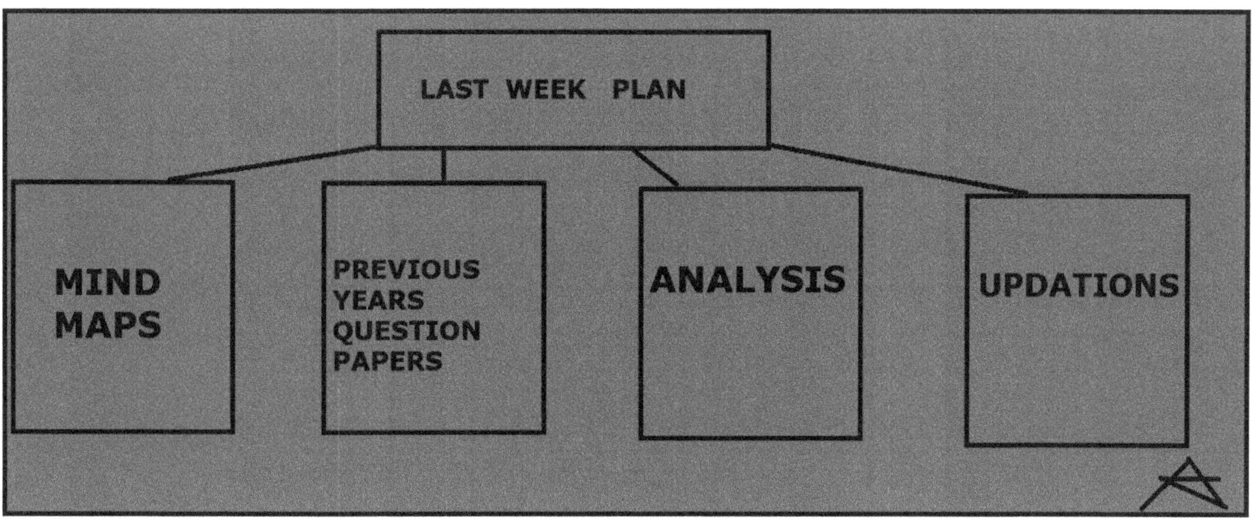

FIG. 13.1: LAST WEEK PLAN

13.2:ASPECTS OF CONCERN: during last month we have 4 aspects of concern-

1.MIND MAPS:

Mind maps ensures interconnected information which is easy to retrieve.so every point of syllabus should be transformed in the form of **"MIND MAPS"** and should be revised again & again during last week.

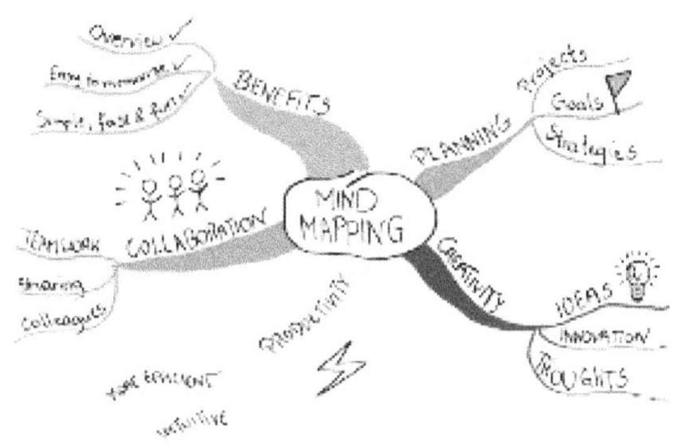

FIG. 13.2: MIND MAPS

2. PREVIOUS YEARS QUESTION PAPERS:

Last week should be used for previous years question papers so that students know exactly what type of questions comes in the exam.so previous years question papers are crucial for gaining self confidence for compeitive exam.

FIG. 13.3: PREVIOUS YEARS QUESTION PAPERS

3.ANALYSIS:

Analysis of your progress is essential for improvement.analyse your mock test results.make a list of your mistakes and rectify them.

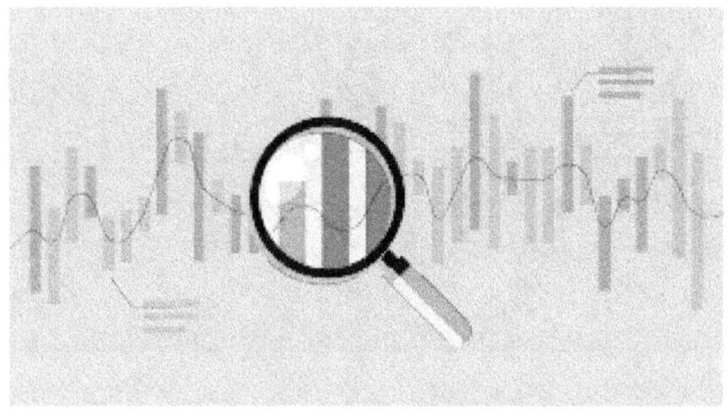

FIG. 13.4: ANALYSIS

4.UPDATIONS:

Update yourself for better performance in exam.

FIG. 13.5: UPDATIONS

CHAPTER FOURTEEN

LAST DAY PLAN

14.1:INTRODUCTION:

Let's discuss the the last day plan.

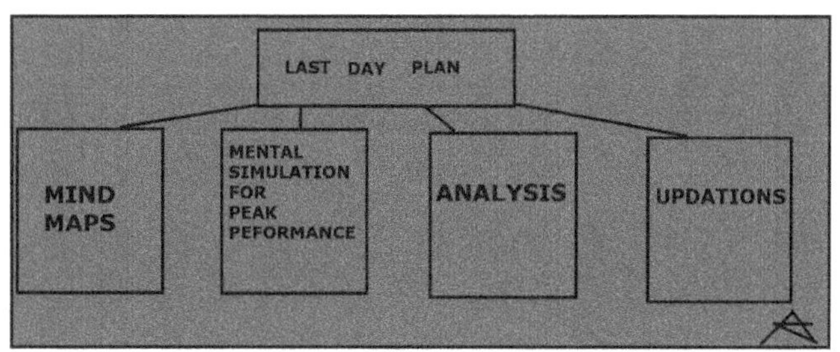

FIG. 14.1: LAST DAY PLAN

14.2:ASPECTS OF CONCERN: during last day we have 4 aspects of concern-

1.MIND MAPS:

Mind maps ensures interconnected information which is easy to retrieve.so every point of syllabus should be transformed in the form of **"MIND MAPS"** and should be revised again & again during last week.

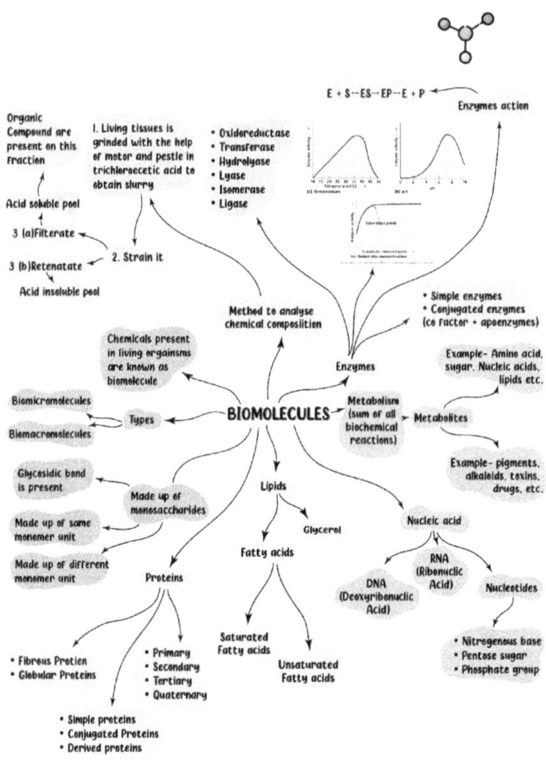

FIG. 14.2: MIND MAPS

2. MENTAL SIMULATION FOR PEAK PERFORMANCE:

Last day should be used for mental simulation for peak performance so that students can practice mentally for exam environment before actual exam.hold yourself at optimal stress level and maintain yourself in this state for 1.5 times the exam duration.for example if your exam has aduration of 3 hours you should practice for 4.5 hours.

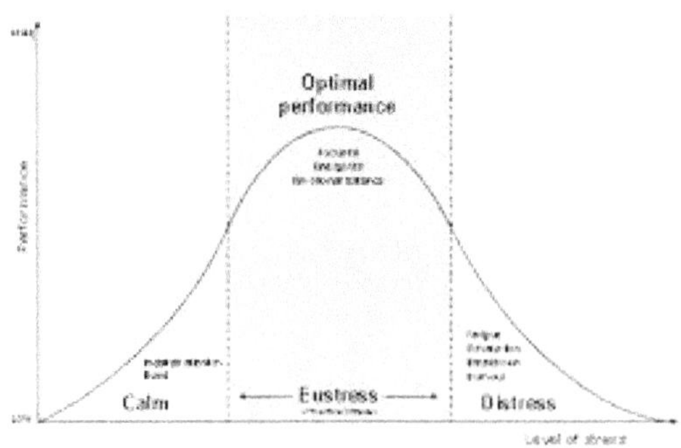

FIG. 14.3: PERFORMANCE VERSUS STRESS GRAPH

FIG. 14.4: MENTAL SIMULATION FOR PEAK PERFORMANCE

3.ANALYSIS:

Analysis of your progress is essential for improvement.analyse your mental simulations,specially learn to cope up with negative emotions like fear,anxiety,hurry etc.learn how to be internally silent & powerful.

FIG. 14.5: ANALYSIS

4.UPDATIONS:

Update yourself so that you can perform better in exam.

FIG. 14.6: UPDATE

CHAPTER FIFTEEN

LAST HOUR PLAN

15.1:INTRODUCTION:

The last hour is extremly crucial for success in competitive exam.make sure that you have an optimal stress level.hold yourself at this stress level by using strong will power.

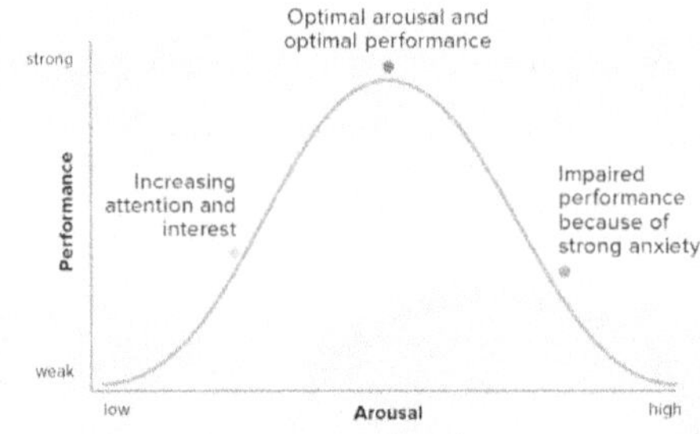

FIG. 15.1: OPTIMAL PERFORMANCE IS AT OPTIMAL STRESS

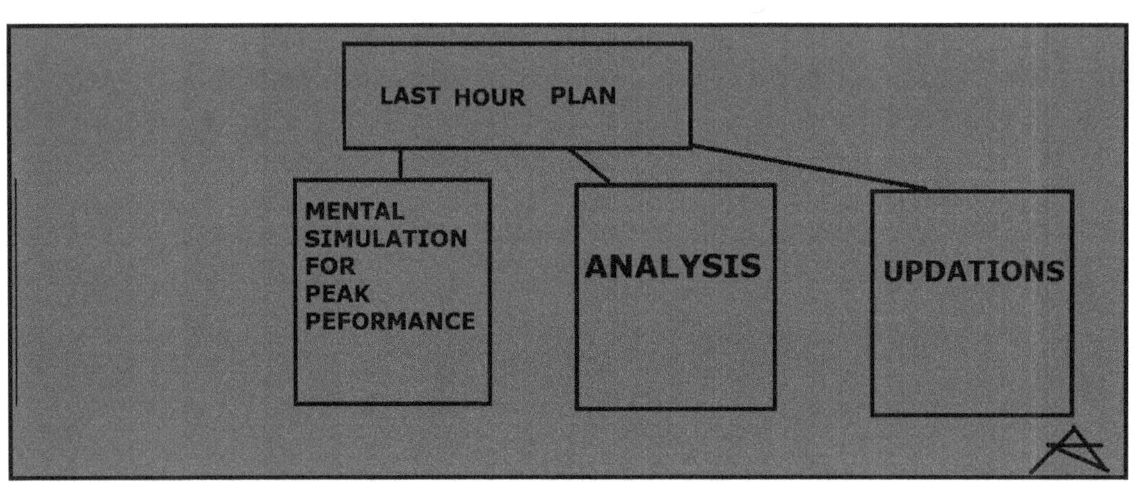

FIG. 15.2: LAST HOUR PLAN

15.2:ASPECTS OF CONCERN: during last day we have 3 aspects of concern-

1. MENTAL SIMULATION FOR PEAK PERFORMANCE:

Last hour should be used for mental simulation for peak performance so that students can practice mentally for exam environment before actual exam.

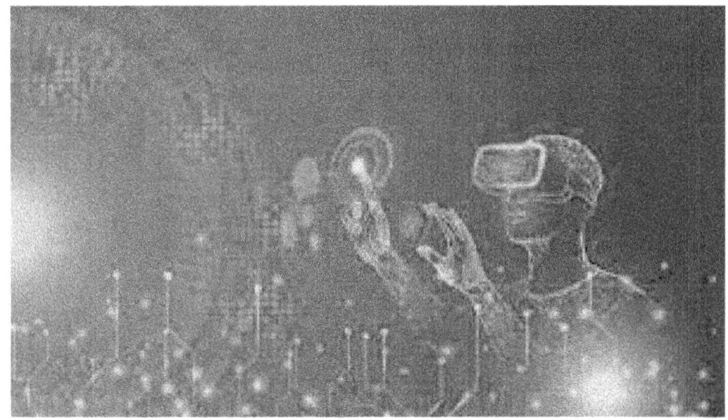

FIG. 15.3: MENTAL SIMULATION

3.ANALYSIS:

Analyse your emotions like fear,anxiety,hurry,excitement etc.learn how to be internally silent & relaxed.operate yourself at optimal stress level.

FIG. 15.4: MENTAL SIMULATION

4.UPDATIONS:

Update your strategies so that you can perform better in exam.

FIG. 15.5: UPDATIONS

CHAPTER SIXTEEN

LAST MINUTE PLAN

16.1: INTRODUCTION:

Last minute plan involves mental simulation & analysis.be internally silent & thoughtless.There should be no reactions to your emotions.be a **neutral observer** and **don't react**.

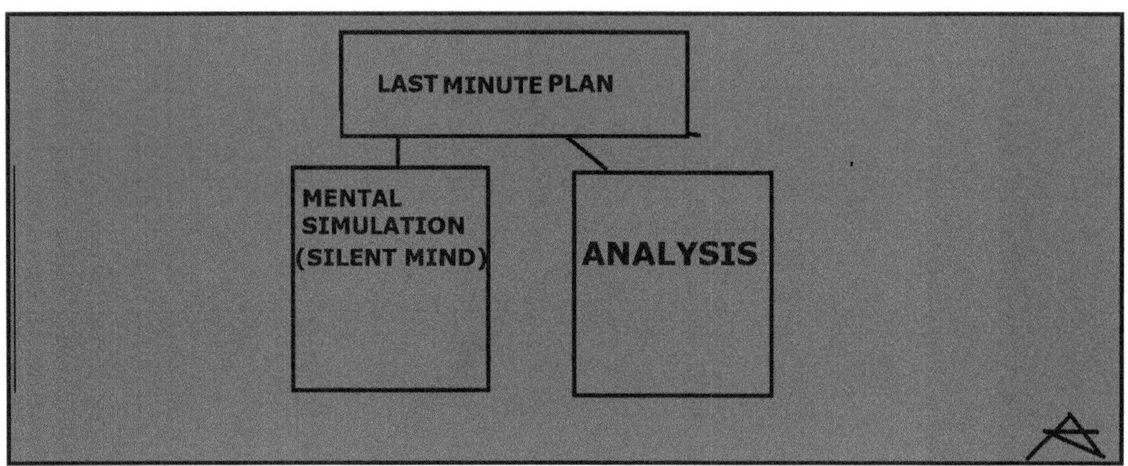

FIG. 16.1: LAST MINUTE PLAN

FIG. 16.2: BE INTERNALLY SILENT

FIG. 16.3: BE A NEUTRAL OBSERBER

FIG. 16.4: BE THOUGHTLESS

16.2:ASPECTS OF CONCERN: during last minute we have 2 aspects of concern-
1. MENTAL SIMULATION FOR SILENT MIND:
Last minute should be used for mental simulation for silent mind.Generally our mind is in reactive state.we react to thougths and are either in past or imagining future.for optimal performance we must be focused at present.Being in a state of silent mind ensures that we are not reacting to past nor imagining future. so that students can practice mentally for exam environment before actual exam.

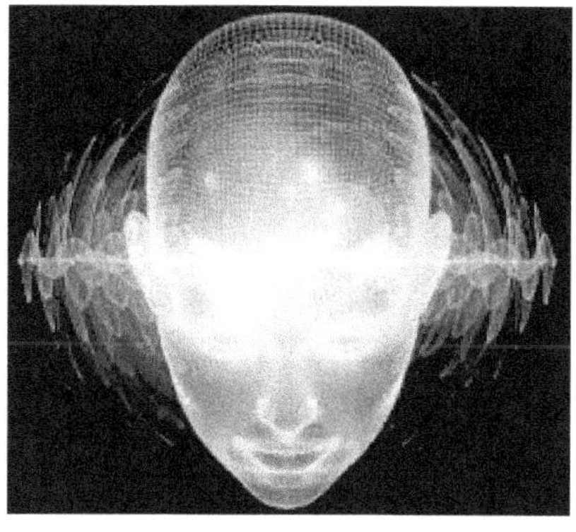

FIG. 16.5: MENTAL SIMULATION FOR SILENT MIND

FIG. 16.6: HUMAN MIND IS TRAPPED IN PAST

FIG. 16.7: HUMAN MIND IS TRAPPED IN FUTURE

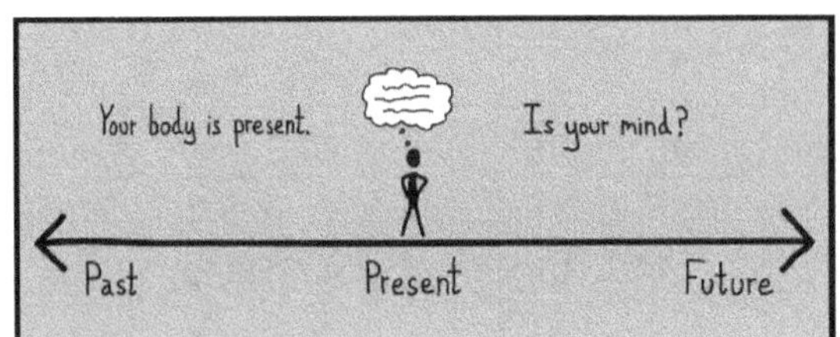

FIG. 16.8: HUMAN MIND IS WANDERING BETWEEN PRESENT,PAST & FUTURE

FIG. 16.9: FOCUS AT PRESENT FOR A BETTER FUTURE

16.3.ANALYSIS:

Analyse your state of mind with a silent mind.

FIG. 16.9: ANALYSIS

CHAPTER SEVENTEEN

LAST SECOND PLAN

17.1:INTRODUCTION:

Last second plan is last but not the least moment of concern.focus on silent state of mind.be in active state of mind.

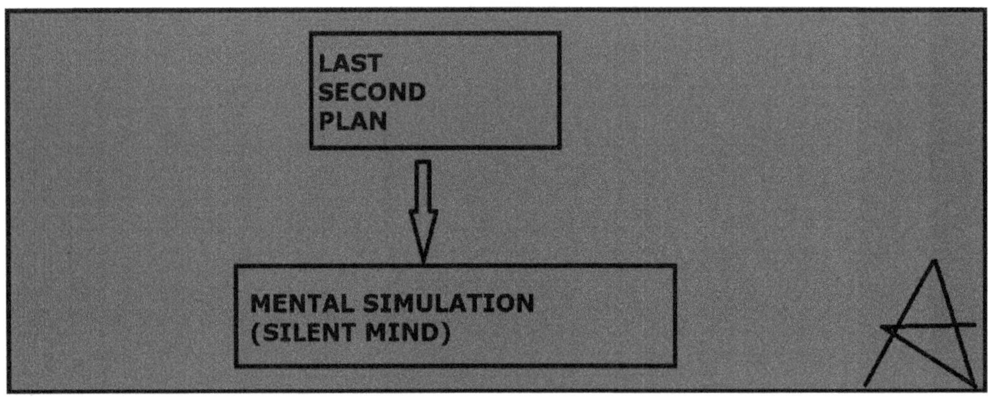

FIG. 17.1: LAST SECOND PLAN

FIG. 17.2: LAST SECOND PLAN

17.2:ASPECTS OF CONCERN: during last second we have only 1 aspects of concern-
MENTAL SIMULATION FOR SILENT MIND:

Last second should be used for mental simulation for silent mind.be free of everything.feel the inner silence.universe started from zero so when you starts from inner state of silence you are in the state of zero.you have time to think,analyse,calculate & observe.so in the last second before writing exam you must simulate your mind for being in a state of absolute zero.

FIG. 17.3: SILENT MIND JUST BEFORE STARTING EXAM

CHAPTER EIGHTEEN

CONCLUSION

FIG. 18.1:CONCLUSION

On the basis of discussions in previous chapters, we can conclude that preparing for competitive exams **is not difficult but different**.

There are many ways to start from initial point to final point but out of these only 1 way is concerned with **minimum movement or displacement or efforts.AVA** is just like a **GPS** to guide you to find the optimal way which requires minimum efforts & optimal/maximum output.

FIG. 18.2: DISPLACEMENT IS THE OPTIMAL PATH

It's my self realisation based on my experience of my own preparation of JEE,which helped me to crack **JEE(M)/AIEEE** with a decent rank & getting selected in government college of technology,pantnagar,uttrakhand, & training thousands of students to crack JEE & NEET in reputed coaching institutes of KOTA & DELHI that if you learn AVA.you can optimise your preparation and can actually prepare for competitive exams rather than struggling with information,thoughts & emotions.

best of luck

Acharya vishvendra

(Av sir)

we have tried our best to keep this book error free.however human efforts are never perfect.there are always chances of errors.if readers find any error they are requested to send us the errors or any issue with the contents of this book at our official e-mail id:vishvendrasir@optimalsuccesstrajectory.org

Enter Caption